GROWING UP QUEER

CRITICAL PERSPECTIVES ON YOUTH

General Editors: Amy L. Best, Lorena Garcia, and Jessica K. Taft

This series aims to elaborate a set of theoretical and methodological tenets for a distinctive critical youth studies approach rooted in empirical inquiry. The series draws upon the following as some of the key theoretical elements of critical approaches: the socially constructed nature of childhood and adolescence over and against the universalizing and naturalizing propensities of early developmental theory; the centering of young people's social worlds and social locations as the starting point for analysis; exploration of how the meaning and experience of youth is shaped by other important axes of social difference, including but not limited to race, class, gender, place, nation, and sexuality; the recognition that youth's worlds are constituted through multiple processes, institutions, and discourses and that central to understanding youth identity and experience is understanding social inequalities; engagement with the dynamics of global transformation in the experience of childhood and youth; and the relevance of these elements for policy and practice.

Books in the series:

Fast-Food Kids: French Fries, Lunch Lines, and Social Ties
Amy L. Best

White Kids: Growing Up with Privilege in a Racially Divided America
Margaret A. Hagerman

Growing Up Queer: Kids and the Remaking of LGBTQ Identity
Mary Robertson

Growing Up Queer

Kids and the Remaking of LGBTQ Identity

Mary Robertson

NEW YORK UNIVERSITY PRESS

New York

NEW YORK UNIVERSITY PRESS
New York
www.nyupress.org

References to Internet websites (URLs) were accurate at the time of writing. Neither the author nor New York University Press is responsible for URLs that may have expired or changed since the manuscript was prepared.

Library of Congress Cataloging-in-Publication Data
Names: Robertson, Mary, author.
Title: Growing up queer : kids and the remaking of LGBTQ identity / Mary Robertson.
Description: New York : New York University Press, [2019] | Series: Critical perspectives on youth | Includes bibliographical references and index.
Identifiers: LCCN 2018020939| ISBN 9781479879601 (cl : alk. paper) | ISBN 9781479876945 (pb : alk. paper)
Subjects: LCSH: Sexual minority youth—United States. | Gay youth—United States. | Sexual minorities—Identity. | Gays—Identity.
Classification: LCC HQ76.27.Y68 R63 2019 | DDC 306.7608350973—dc23
LC record available at https://lccn.loc.gov/2018020939

New York University Press books are printed on acid-free paper, and their binding materials are chosen for strength and durability. We strive to use environmentally responsible suppliers and materials to the greatest extent possible in publishing our books.

Manufactured in the United States of America

10 9 8 7 6 5 4 3 2 1

Also available as an ebook

For Patrick,

whose generosity of time and spirit

has touched so many lives

CONTENTS

Introduction

"A Whole Lot of Queer"

And then I finally went there, and it was all colorful and magical. Full of hope. . . . And then, I remember just the queerness of it. Like, seeing genderqueers and butches and flaming gay guys, it was just a whole lot of queer. . . . I feel like this is like my family here. Like literally, my family. I haven't felt this close with people ever in my life [*laughs*]. I come here and you feel the love, you feel the energy, everyone knows everyone. . . . The only time and space in my life where I actually get to truly relax and enjoy myself and the people around me and just laugh.
—Zia, nineteen-year-old, identifies as queer, racially mixed, and Black, describing her first visit to Spectrum at fifteen years old

In September 2010, I visit The Resource, the LGBTQ center in my community, for the first time. It has quite literally just opened its doors at its new location.[1] After many years occupying the second floor of a retail building a few miles away, The Resource had raised the funds to buy a new building, renovated it to meet LEED certification, and taken its rightful, visible place as a fundamental community leader in this gentrifying gayborhood.[2] Part of city-sponsored main street redevelopment, the building—cube-shaped with a rooftop garden and modern architectural flourishes like charcoal-colored brick and white louvers—comes right up to the sidewalk along one of the busiest avenues in town. There is a large sign on the corner that says "The Resource," the colors of the rainbow subtly suggesting the mission of the organization. This busy corner is a mix of residential apartments, old Victorian homes, coffee shops, business offices, tattoo parlors, thrift stores, bars, and restaurants.

The street is busy with cars, buses, bicyclists, and pedestrians twenty-four hours a day.

I arrive in the heat of the afternoon sun and wait in the parking lot in front of the building to meet my friend, Michael, who volunteers at Spectrum—The Resource's LGBTQ youth drop-in center. I've asked Michael to introduce me to Spectrum with the intention of it being a field site for some exploratory research I'm doing on vulnerable youth and sexuality. Today I'll see the space, meet some of the staff and youth, and get the chance to pitch my project to the program manager. I'm a little bit nervous, hesitating to go in by myself without Michael. I've never been to The Resource or Spectrum before, mainly because I'm not gay. I am relatively familiar with the organization as a community resource, but I simply never had a reason to come here before. As I wait I become aware of how, simply by being here, others are likely to think I *am* gay. This brief foray outside my bubble of hetero privilege gets me thinking about all of the ways we attribute sexual orientation or identity onto others, association with queer organizations being but one. It also occurs to me that, owing to the stigma attached to queer spaces, it must not be easy for a young person, in the midst of trying to figure out their sexuality, to come here for the first time. Now that I am here, the thought of entering a room full of teenagers is kind of giving me a heart attack. It feels a bit like the first day at a new school. Will the kids like me? Will I fit in? Am I wearing the right thing? Will they trust me? This anxiety about belonging, intention, and trust will inform much of my time here at Spectrum over the next few years.

I am profoundly self-conscious of my own sexual orientation as I embark on this project. I was a women's studies major and feminist activist in college when I first began, in earnest, the lifelong process of reckoning with my privilege, a process that has made me hyper aware of my identities and how I present in various identity-based groups and that leads me to always question my actions, thoughts, and assumptions. On my college campus I organized against war, racism, homophobia, and sexism alongside LGBTQ-identified friends and colleagues. But I know enough about how privilege works to understand that no matter how conscious I am, as a person living with multiple intersecting forms of privilege I'm still likely to reproduce inequality as often as I succeed at dismantling it. I am very anxious about entering an LGBTQ space as a person with heterosexual and cisgender privilege with the intention of conducting research, so much so that when I fill out the paperwork to become a volunteer and email it to the program manager, I mention that I had been awarded the Ally of the Year Award by the Pride center in college. To me, this award is proxy for my LGBTQ credentials.

My anticipation is not due to being unfamiliar with LGBTQ-identified people and spaces. Nor am I uncomfortable with being labeled LGBTQ. Given my somewhat butch self-presentation, my feminist activist identity, and my general disdain for traditional gender roles, I am likely often assigned that label by others regardless. Yet, much like when a lesbian friend of mine in college christened me an "honorary lesbian," my anxiety stems from a sense of being down for the cause but not quite belonging. This old, familiar feeling stewed in me as I waited for Michael in the parking lot. As well intentioned as it was, the "honorary lesbian" title always rubbed me the wrong way because I didn't need to be a lesbian to embrace what it means to be queer. Yet, as a ciswoman involved in a long-term intimate partnership with a man, I could in no way claim an authentic lesbian (or LGBTQ) identity.

The notion of an honorary lesbian, however, is a useful way to think about how we become sexual. In most ways, I qualified in my friend's eyes as lesbian, yet I didn't identify as one, and I was having sex with a man. So what were the lines I followed that led me to desire men, and how did I learn them?[3] Is it in fact true that I do not inherently desire women, or is it more the case that the variety of ways I exist in the world, the pressures I experience, the examples I am given have led me toward my particular sexual orientations? Had I come of age at a different time, in a different place, with different options, would I still be heterosexually oriented? Exactly what characteristics would make me a real lesbian? This is the starting place for this book: Given the context of their lives, how do teenagers become sexual and gendered today? Recognizing that not all young people share the same contexts, I explore how the very particular context of the lives of the kids of Spectrum matters to their becoming.

Queer Orientations

Through my ethnographic research at Spectrum, including participant observation and life history interviews with young people, I argue that the space and most of the people I met there are queerly oriented. I show how Spectrum is an example of queerness and explain why, in the context of twenty-first-century sexuality and gender politics, making the distinction between queer and a more mainstream understanding of LGBTQ continues to be valuable. As more and more young people are self-identifying as LGBTQ, queer, trans*, gender fluid, and a myriad of other identities related to gender and sexuality, the term "LGBTQ youth" has become commonplace; there appears to be consensus that we all know what an LGBTQ youth is. Of course, "LGBTQ" is a useful term to denote a collective, marginalized identity based on sexuality and gender (one I use liberally throughout this book), but I will push the reader to think in a more complicated way about what exactly LGBTQ means and represents. To tell the story of how one forms their sexuality is not just about sexual desire and conduct. It is also the story of becoming gendered, forming identities within a particular social, historical, and cultural context and representation and recognition within family, media, and community.

In an interview with Ernie, a twenty-one-year-old Chicanx who identifies as queer, he tells me that, when he speaks of gay and queer, "It's, like, two different things." I press him for more and he goes on:

> The gay, what I call the "gay crowd" or the "gay movement" is um, gay people that are trying to like become mainstream and . . . how could we be, look as normal as possible? When we as queer people are . . . gender is fluid, sexual orientation is fluid . . . we don't have to be as normal or like date one person or date this person because of their gender expressions, like we're more fluid about things. And yeah, and I think that's a big difference, where the gay movement tries to be like more mainstream.

He describes the LGBTQ movement as a gay movement, pointing to the fact that it is represented by gay, white males. He also emphasizes that he finds the gay rights movement to be exclusive, one that does not concern itself with the rights of women, people of color, and trans-identified people: "And I think the . . . the queer movement . . . does come together with other movements, whereas the gay movement kind of doesn't, it's like, they stick to themselves more." I asked if he thought Spectrum was more of a gay space or a queer space, which led to this explanation of how Spectrum differs from The Resource:

> The Resource is gay. . . . It's very like, "How normal can we be? How like, heteronormative can we be?" But once you go down them stairs and open that Spectrum door, it gets as queer as fuck. Like . . . it's really queer. And like, it's just something amazing where you . . . just see like, people trying on different shit and just exploring everything and, yeah it's just really, I think as a, how do you say, organization? It's really split between everything like, age, and everything. Like the age difference? You can tell the difference. Like, upstairs it's like very, very gay and downstairs it's like, really queer and I'm like, I hope I don't become gay like them [*laughs*].

Spectrum, quite obviously, is a queer space because of its recognition and validation of non-heteronormative sexualities and genders. But also critical to my argument here (and Ernie's) is that Spectrum's queerness also has to do with how the youth exist in opposition to mainstream conceptions of normal *beyond* sexuality and gender. The youth of Spectrum, contrary to popular media depictions of LGBTQ youth, are not like the television cast of *Glee!*, a group of pitch-perfect, attractive, happy theater geeks. The youth are more likely to refer to themselves as "Little Monsters," a term of endearment coined by the mega pop star Lady Gaga to refer to her queer fans. One's access to "normal" depends on race, class, ability, citizenship, language, geography, education, skills, and more. Among the queer people of Spectrum are youth of color; the poor and working-class; undocumented migrants; those involved in the criminal legal system; people living with physical, cognitive, and intellectual disabilities; high school dropouts; kids experiencing homelessness; and socially awkward nerds obsessed with Japanese *anime* and *Buffy the Vampire Slayer*. Very few Spectrum youth are white, middle-class kids with access to resources. And while the youth all gather here under the banner of LGBTQ, same-sex sexual desire and/or trans* experience is not necessarily something they all have in common. Queer is what they have in common.

Throughout this book, I use the feminist scholar Sara Ahmed's concept of "queer orientation" to make my argument that this is not a universal story about LGBTQ youth but, rather, one about queer youth specifically. Following Ahmed, I use "queer" both to describe a way of being in the world that opposes normal (sometimes intentionally, sometimes not), as well as to describe sexual conduct and behavior. Therefore, not all heterosexual sexualities are normal and not all LGBTQ-identified people are queer. One can be queerly oriented because they resist the straightening effects of the dominant culture or because one's queerness results in being disallowed access to straightness. A queer orientation explains how people and bodies can be *made* queer by society—"Some of us more than others, look wonky"—or people can choose queer by self-determination.[4] To have a queer orientation is both how some are seen by others as different, strange, out of the ordinary, and then labeled as such, and how deviating from straight culture means forging different paths and therefore seeing or orienting toward different things. Of course, one's experience might be some combination of both.

Queer orientation is a useful tool to understand sexualities and genders for several reasons. First, it moves away from the bioessentialist/ social constructionist debate, where sexuality and gender are either something one is born with or something one learns, making room for a more nuanced understanding of both. Second, it encourages a conversation about a diversity of experience among those with marginalized and stigmatized sexualities and genders rather than universalizing varied experiences. Third, it works to distinguish sexual *behavior* from sexual *identities*. In an effort to explain sexual orientation outside of a bioessentialist framework, Ahmed argues, "In the case of sexual orientation, it is not simply that we have it. . . . Certain objects are available to us because of lines that we have already taken: our life courses follow a certain sequence, which is also a matter of following a direction or being directed in a certain way. . . . The concept of orientations allows us to expose how life gets directed through the very requirement that we follow what is already given to us."[5] Put another way, sexual desire may feel innate to the individual experiencing it, but the possibilities of straightness and queerness are products of our social world, not equally available to all. How one expresses their sexual desire and how others interpret that expression are influenced by gender and other identity categories like race, class, and ability; cultural conditions such as family, religion, and geographical location; and social institutions like media, education, and law.

The work here fills a niche in the area of youth sexualities by exploring, in particular, how young people *become* sexual, whereas much of the existing research takes for granted the a priori existence of sexual orientation and identity. This book expands on sociological theories of sexuality and gender as social constructions using queer theory to demonstrate the significance of queer orientation. This is important because, if the move away from bioessentialist understandings of sexuality and toward an acceptance of sexual and gender fluidity is a lasting trend, there are significant sociological implications in the areas of sex and gender, sexualities, and social movements.

Beyond Risk or Resilience

As I began volunteering at Spectrum in the fall of 2010, the sex advice columnist and gay activist Dan Savage kicked off the now famous "It Gets Better" campaign in response to a rash of suicides among LGBTQ youth that was gaining national attention at the time. The media response to Savage's social media campaign placed a national spotlight on LGBTQ youth, and Spectrum was abuzz with discussion about these events. While Sid, Spectrum's program manager, and César, the then program coordinator, were on the one hand supportive of the youths' excitement about campaigns like "It Gets Better," on the other they were skeptical of the media's focus on the precarity of LGBTQ youth. Too often the media paint a dreary picture of the plight of LGBTQ youth, which both adds to the already depressing climate these young people face and erases the constructive, positive contributions they make to society.

The dominant discourse about LGBTQ youth is that they occupy a state of crisis. In a virulently homophobic society, their sexual and gender minority status results in endless incidents of bullying and discrimination by others and an insidious internalized homophobia that manifests itself in high rates of self-harm. Yet Sid and César were quick to point out that just because LGBTQ youth suicide was currently getting a lot of attention in the media did not mean it was a new phenomenon. Their point was that LGBTQ youth have been struggling *and* surviving for a long time. Therefore the program managers aimed to broadcast a different ideology about these young people. Their emphasis was on empowering the youth community to care for itself, rather than depending on outsiders to "save" it. Sid emphasized the following point frequently to the youths of Spectrum: "We don't need anyone to come save us; we need people to follow our lead and support us." She explained that the queer community is fierce and not just composed of victims who get bullied and kill themselves.

In his article, "Young, Gay, and Suicidal," sociologist Tom Waidzunas explains that too often, master narratives about LGBTQ youth are either stories of precarity or resiliency. On the matter of suicide rates among LGBTQ youth, he argues, "While efforts to address the issue of gay youth suicide from both risk and resilience perspectives clearly reflect immense concern about gay teens, both approaches have often given way to coarse generalization due to the need for strong claims in public policy disputes. . . . As long as researchers adhere to broad brush claims, the subtleties, complexities, and nuances of LGBTQ youth experiences will remain obfuscated by sweeping generalizations."[6] In response to this critique, *Growing Up Queer* attempts to dispel universal assumptions about the LGBTQ youth subject by telling a more particular story about queer-oriented young people and queer spaces.

The developmental psychologist Ritch Savin-Williams, one of the most prolific researchers on LGBTQ youth, makes a convincing argument in his 2007 book, *The New Gay Teenager*, that teenagers today are not preoccupied with sexual orientation in the same way that older generations have been. He suggests we are experiencing "the integration and normalization of homoeroticism, resulting in the near disappearance of the gay adolescent and the emergence of sexually diverse young people."[7] Like Waidzunas, he argues that many of the discourses of precarity that surround LGBTQ youth result in a misrepresentation of all gay youths' experiences. Savin-Williams points out that much of what we know about this youth population is based on research done with people who are frequenting largely urban LGBTQ centers with youth programs (like Spectrum) or youth who were in one way or another state supervised. Therefore the subject population under study is not representative of the LGBTQ youth population at large, meaning the research does not likely include those youth who—because of intersecting forms of privilege, disposition, and circumstance—are not congregating in youth centers. In other words, Savin-Williams's work suggests that the runaway, suicidal, self-harming LGBTQ youth is over-represented in the study samples, while the gay kid who is crowned prom king and off to an Ivy League college is underrepresented.

The sociologist C. J. Pascoe has a related finding in her ethnographic study of high school kids, *Dude, You're a Fag*, published around the same time as the *New Gay Teenager*. Pascoe shows how the fag discourse is used by adolescent boys as a tool to police masculinity. While the boys in her study constantly call each other out for "acting gay," they know it is mean to tease boys who actually identify as gay. Gay boys and men are largely accepted, as long as they act manly enough. It is different for Ricky, the *queer* kid in the school who *is* actually bullied for his gender and sexuality—not just teased or policed by his buddies. Pascoe explains, "While boys at River High engaged in continual repudiatory rituals around fag identity, Ricky embodied the fag because of his homosexuality and his less normative gender identification and self-presentation."[8] Ricky, who had suffered a lifetime of homophobic bullying by students, teachers, and administrators while attending various schools, dropped out of River High by the time Pascoe left her field site. His sexuality and gender were not normal enough. My work continues in a similar vein to Savin-Williams's and Pascoe's in that it aims to complicate the LGBTQ youth subject; Savin-William's argument, that homoeroticism is normalized among youth today, and Pascoe's argument, that queer sexualities and genders continue to be policed, are simultaneously accurate. I argue that treating all so-called LGBTQ youth as one collapsible category results in over-simplifying the normalization of homoeroticism and obscuring the nuanced difference between homonormative and queer LGBTQ-identified kids.

Sexuality Research in Queer Spaces

Our understanding of sexuality from a research standpoint is incomplete without a complex exploration of child and youth sexualities. Yet owing to the pervasiveness of sex-negative cultural frameworks in the United States, it is very difficult for sexualities researchers to gain access to minors. Entrenched conservative ideologies about childhood sexual innocence, abstinence-only-until-marriage pseudo-sex education curriculums, and homophobic, misogynist, heterosexist assumptions about sexuality have kept accurate information about sexuality out of schools and away from young people and prevent various institutions from allowing—much less encouraging—research on youth sexualities.[9]

Given this cultural climate, it is no wonder that the research that is centered on youth sexualities overemphasizes so-called risk behaviors among marginalized populations like girls, LGBTQ-identified youth, and youth of color.[10] Individuals who occupy these various identities and their intersections are sexually suspect in a heteropatriarchal society in which the only form of acceptable sexuality is heterosexual, reproductive, and driven by male desire. Therefore, in addition to the need for a better understanding of sexual subjectivity, there is also a need for a sociology of the center, where dominant sexualities come under scrutiny in the same ways that marginalized sexualities have.

Yet there is an interesting paradox at work here. The sexualities of those who are most marginalized, whose behaviors, identities, and desires are seen as the most atypical, are often most visible and accessible to researchers. For example, the fact that our culture holds girls and women (and gay men) largely responsible for sexual health, including pregnancy and sexually transmitted infection prevention, means that sexual health resources like reproductive health clinics are gendered female. And, unlike access to a school classroom—where a researcher might gain access to an array of sexualities, including those most privileged in society—access to a health clinic often results in a gender-biased account of the story.[11]

Similarly, because LGBTQ-identified people have had to seek support and resources outside of dominant cultural institutions—like schools—LGBTQ resource centers, which operate on the periphery and have had to be at the forefront of sexual health crises like HIV/AIDS, have become some of the most progressive sources of sexual information in U.S. culture.[12] Further, I found that the adult staff members of Spectrum were not afraid to talk frankly with young people about their sexuality, and both The Resource and Spectrum were welcoming to researchers because they supported the need for strong, evidence-based data related to LGBTQ issues. While I understand the importance of a sociology of the center when it comes to better understanding sexuality, because of the constraints described here, an LGBTQ-youth resource center—as opposed to a public school, for example—was the most ideal location for me to explore sexual subjectivity with young people. I argue that the LGBTQ community occupies the leading edge of the development and dissemination of sexual health practices, many of which are eventually adopted by the mainstream, making sexuality healthier, happier, and more fun for everyone. Rather than see my focus on marginalized sexualities as a weakness, I hope to show the promise and possibility of queer youth culture and its potential to influence sexuality and gender broadly.

Sociology of Sexualities and Queer Theory

My research and analysis is largely informed by a combination of the sociology of sexualities and queer theory. Sociologists and queer theorists have provided ample evidence that gender and sexuality are constructed categories, but the larger public discourse on homosexuality continues to be one based on essentialism.[13] Within the LGBTQ rights movement, strategic essentialism—organizing around the idea that one is born gay—has been a powerful framework within which a civil rights battle has been fought and is largely being won.[14] Yet sociologists of sexuality and queer theorists have long been arguing that sexual identities and the meanings attached to homosexuality, heterosexuality, and bisexuality are socially and historically contingent.[15] Social constructionism and queer theory applied to LGBTQ identity has resulted in a conundrum of sorts. If sexuality (and, equally important, gender) is a social and historical—not biological—fact, sexual orientation and identity become slippery social positions to occupy and organize. Queer activism and theory have provided a counter to the essentialist discourse both within the LGBTQ rights movement and academia. Queer theory questions the logic of an essentialist discourse and argues for a dismantling of sex and gender binaries. As the evidence provided throughout this book shows, the ideas and challenges to bioessentialism that have been articulated by the queer movement are successfully disrupting normative ideas about sexuality and gender among the youth of Spectrum.

My analysis is informed by queer theorists like Gayle Rubin, Adrienne Rich, and Michael Warner, whose explorations of heterosexual dominance in society have led to what is becoming a more and more widely understood concept: heteronormativity.[16] I use "heteronormativity" throughout to refer to the various ways that the naturalization of heterosexuality as normal results in both the marginalization of all non-heterosexual forms of sexuality and desire and essentialized understandings of binary masculinity and femininity. Further, my work also relies on the concept of heteropatriarchy, which acknowledges how both heterosexual and male supremacist ideologies work hand in hand to maintain capitalist, colonialist systems of oppression in society. In particular, I rely on the sociologist Roderick Ferguson's interpretation of the "queer-of-color analysis," informed by women of color feminism and queer and poststructuralist theories, that "interrogates social formations as the intersections of race, gender, sexuality, and class, with particular interest in how those formations correspond with and diverge from nationalist ideals and practices."[17] Therefore, beyond simply challenging heteronormative concepts of sexuality and gender, the queer-of-color analysis exposes how these characteristics function within racialized and classed systems of power. Sexuality has been used as a tool to justify the dehumanization of the racialized other in a patriarchal, white supremacist U.S. culture.[18] Therefore any exploration of adolescent sexualities or marginalized sexualities must take race, class, nationality, and other social categories into account because of the various ways sexuality is interpreted through the lens of power.

Reflecting on My Own Identities

Although it is common and accepted behavior to share your *gender* identity—via pronouns—with the Spectrum community almost as soon as you arrive in the space, it is a bit taboo to ask or announce one's *sexual* identity until more personal, intimate relationships develop. Because of this, people in the space are likely to know that I use female gender pronouns but are not always aware that I identify as straight. The staff and many of the youth who are around a lot are more likely to know more about my sexual identity largely because of the way small details about one's personal life trickle out in day-to-day conversation. But otherwise, I could never be sure how people at Spectrum perceived my sexual identity.

All of us at Spectrum, socialized in a heteronormative culture, make assumptions about people's sexual identity based on the language we use to talk about ourselves—for instance, my use of the word "partner" to describe my intimate companion. I use this term on purpose as a way to resist the patriarchal, gendered implications of words like "boyfriend" or "husband" and "girlfriend" or "wife," and among some company, it may signal a same-sex or queer relationship. We also make assumptions about people's sexual identity by observing the various ways one performs their gender. Does my short hair and boyish style of dress get me read as lesbian? But these assumptions—which are based largely on gender stereotypes—are often unreliable. For example, Michael, who has identified as a gay man since he was an adolescent, has an unambiguously masculine gender expression. He makes no effort to present as a man—he has little interest in his clothing choices beyond comfort and sensibility and is not concerned with maintaining a hypermasculine physique—yet his voice is masculine sounding and he has no feminine secondary/tertiary characteristics that are often associated with gayness among men. I learned both from talking to him and from my own interactions with youth that it is common for youths to assume Michael is straight based on how he looks and acts. He doesn't act gay. In this way Michael stands out compared to the other adult gay men in the space, all of whom look or act "more gay" than he does.

Along these lines, two occasions when my sexuality was called into question by youth stand out to me. I was talking about the upcoming queer prom with Matthew, one of the youths I interviewed and knew quite well. I said my partner, Robert, was coming with me to the dance, and when I said my partner's name, Matthew sort of stopped and said, "Wait, so are you straight?" This information was clearly something he had to process, and I could tell as we sat there that it was causing him to retool his image of me.

The other occasion was with Alex. I had just completed an interview with him, turned off the tape recorder, and was wrapping up. I always end by asking interviewees if they have any questions for me. He said he wanted to ask me something. He hesitated for quite some time, reassuring me that my answer "[didn't] really matter" but that he was just really curious and wanted to know something. Finally he asked, "Are you gay?" Alex's reluctance to ask me about my sexual identity is a good example of how within Spectrum it was not considered "polite" to ask people about their sexual identity. As he struggled with wanting so badly to know this information about me, he simultaneously struggled with his insistence that it does not really matter. Yet it does matter.

Although all of the full-time staff identify as gay, lesbian, or queer, there are straight student interns and peer staff, as well as a small number of straight youth who use the space, so being straight at Spectrum was not wildly unusual. But there is no mechanism at Spectrum for individuals to publicly identify their sexual identity. While Michael was misread as straight because he does not fit a gay male stereotype, I was misread as LGBTQ by Matthew, who appeared surprised to learn I was straight. Reflecting on the various cues we all use—absent full disclosure—to guess at someone's sexual identity, both Matthew's and Alex's interest in my sexuality reveals a process of boundary making that occurs within the walls of Spectrum. This process is an example of becoming sexual that has little to do with sexual behavior and conduct and much to do with forming meaning around identity and desire. In most social interactions outside spaces like Spectrum, though, the tables are turned, where the scrutiny is on the person with a queer sexuality, not a straight one.

Straightness is not constructed in the same manner as gayness. There is no parallel experience of sexual self-realization for heterosexual-oriented persons to that of those who *identify* otherwise. For it is not same-sex desire or same-sex behavior that makes one gay any more than it is the absence of same-sex desire or behavior that makes one straight. Rather, the maintenance of a binary sexual order is a co-constitutive process in which a rejection of heteronormativity requires an explanation, while maintaining straightness does not. Persons whose sexual desires are largely in line with heterosexuality do not have to account for their desires and behaviors—heterosexual or homosexual—the way those whose desires are not. Further, self-understanding only goes so far, since others will ascribe or attribute a sexual identity to you based on your gendered behavior and expression, regardless of whether it accurately describes your sexuality. And in my attempts to describe the youth of Spectrum and confound this system of creating difference, I rely on the very markers that I hope will work to convey to the reader some sense of what I see, hear, and notice about these young people. It's a complicated business, to be sure.

The point is to show how unreliable the categories we use to understand each other can be. Take again my status as a straight person. While within Spectrum we can all adopt and disclose sexual identities, one's identity is not a stand-in for desires and behaviors. My straight identity—which is driven largely by being in a long-term, monogamous relationship with a man—does not mean I don't experience homosexual desire or have never engaged in homosexual behavior. Similarly, my interpretations of the youths of Spectrum and their sexualities and genders is limited to what they willingly shared about their identities, desires, and behaviors, along with my attributions and interpretations of them based on what I observed. For many of them, their sexual identities seem to be based more on their gender expression and gendered desires than on actual sexual behavior, which I discuss in chapter 2. Therefore, by looking at adolescent sexualities—which are newly forming, compared to adults—we can ask provocative questions about how sexuality is informed by orientation, desire, behavior, and identity. What is it exactly that counts as sexuality?

Because disclosure of one's specific sexual identity is not expected in LGBTQ spaces, straight allies are not always clearly separated from LGBTQ members of the group. Disclosure requires that group members actively assert their right to membership. Among adolescents, many of whom are not sexually active, figuring out how to claim membership in an LGBTQ community is quite different compared to older people who *have* engaged in homosexuality, are in same-sex intimate relationships, and are more established in their identities. There were members of the Spectrum community who, for example, identified as bisexual or pansexual, yet had only had heterosexual sex or been in other-sex intimate relationships. In other words, one does not have to have engaged in homosexual behavior to self-identify as lesbian, gay, bisexual, or any other non-heterosexual identity. Similarly, having had experiences with homosexuality does not foreclose on a straight identity. Gender works much the same way. While there are many trans*-identified young people at Spectrum who are transitioning to a gender other than that aligned with the sex they were assigned at birth, there are also many who are simply genderqueer. And some who have transitioned from one gender to another are largely unrecognizable to others as a gender that "matches" the sex they were assigned at birth.

My own identities and the ways I am perceived by people at Spectrum are part of the story I tell here. My generally dominant or "normal" social status is often destabilized within the boundaries of the Spectrum community, where what is considered high status differs from the world outside of those boundaries. As the outsider—one who is straight, cisgender, white, of high socioeconomic status, and perhaps most important, an adult—I struggled to communicate effectively in this world of mostly queer teenagers. This is not to suggest, of course, that my power is somehow usurped by the youth of Spectrum, but the work here might illuminate the instability of power. While the social power I possess in the space is significant, it is a mistake to deny the youth of Spectrum their power, too. The dominant and the marginalized are co-constituted.

And it is here that I can begin to destabilize my own claims to normative or dominant status based on the characteristics I used to describe myself above. Although I am all of those things—straight, cis, white, adult, high social status—my personal lived experience within each of those categories is also a queered one. For example, although my partner is a man, being child free and having never married, our family unit is queer within the context of heteronormative relationships; being forty-something adults with no children is decidedly queer.[19] In addition, although I am never mistaken for anything other than an adult among the youth of Spectrum, my rejection of mainstream adult norms when it comes to dress, attitude, and behavior marked me as a different kind of adult within the space. Youth often expressed great surprise when they learned my actual age. I was able to adopt a "least-adult" role because as a researcher I could sidestep much of the disciplinary roles that other adults in the space had to perform.[20] Rather than supervise while the youth of Spectrum played Lip Sync for Your Life, an impromptu live performance competition popular on the TV show *RuPaul's Drag Race*, or the video game *Guitar Hero*, I participated. While these are just two examples—my queer heterosexuality and adulthood—I hope to remind the reader that, depending on the context, dominant social categories can be queered and queer social categories can be dominant.

Methodological Approach

Spectrum, founded in 1998, is open to young people between the ages of thirteen and twenty-two who identify as LGBTQ and their allies. In addition to being a safe drop-in space, Spectrum has developed daily programming that ranges from art and poetry workshops to sex education and community organizing sessions to a monthly drag show. Spectrum provides snacks, music, access to computers and the internet, health services, counseling and referral, and other resources for youth. Spectrum employs a youth-adult partnership model of service delivery in which youth leaders are trained in peer-based support, safe sex education, and HIV prevention. In an effort to disrupt the power adults have over youths at Spectrum, the youth-adult partnership model helps to ensure that youths hold leadership roles in the space and are actively engaged in some aspects of decision-making processes. During my time there, two full-time adult staff, part-time undergraduate and graduate student interns from the fields of social work and human services, adult volunteers, and peer staff/volunteers ran Spectrum. As previously mentioned, Spectrum operates under the supervision of The Resource, an umbrella organization that provides a wide variety of services to adults in the LGBTQ community.

I didn't set out to do ethnography about an LGBTQ youth center. Spectrum was just one of three field sites where I was doing exploratory fieldwork in preparation for a qualitative study of vulnerability to commercial sexual exploitation. Therefore my research was in pursuit of men and boys who were involved in selling or trading sex, and Spectrum was but one location where I hoped to encounter them. As incongruous as these two topics may seem, connecting my early pursuit—men and boys who sell and trade sex—with the subject of this book—queer youth—is my interest in how sexuality and marginalization interact. I was interested in learning more about how one's race, gender, sexuality, and other socially constructed identities result in marginalization that leads to vulnerability. In the end, the book turned out to be not much about vulnerability and a lot about queerness as a form of marginalization.

After several months of exploratory fieldwork at a homeless youth outreach organization and an intravenous drug user day shelter, along with Spectrum, I had made only three contacts with boys who had experience selling or trading sex; it became obvious that I had to retool my research project. Although all three organizations were rich sites of sociological inquiry, without question the place I most loved to be was Spectrum. I felt more like a member of the Spectrum community than I did the other two communities. Being at Spectrum was putting me in touch with some long-ago forgotten feelings and experiences of my own youth as a queer kid who struggled to find a place for myself in the middle school and high school milieux.

After many years of debilitating depression, my father committed suicide when I was twelve years old. He had exceeded his insurance coverage maximums and that, combined with his inability to work, left my family in financial trouble. My mother, sisters, and I moved out of the neighborhood where I had grown up in to a rental house across town. I was bullied by my best girlfriends *Mean Girls*–style in middle school and arrived in high school with a huge chip on my shoulder about popularity.[21] Although I didn't hang out on the "gay wall" (as described by a Spectrum youth, Fiona, later in the book), my friends were the Freaks. We all smoked cigarettes and pot. The boys had long hair and played guitars instead of sports or wore makeup and solo danced at goth clubs. The girls pierced their ears and noses with needles, cut themselves, and had sex with men much older than we were. I was not outwardly as rebellious as my friends, but my rebellion was formed by my disgust with the mainstream. I didn't want to go off to college to spend another four years with these people who drove me crazy in high school. I didn't want to be a mom. And I definitely did not want to be someone's wife. Many years out of high school, I still feel out of place much of the time. Whereas it's easy to start to feel bad about that, being at Spectrum reminds me of all that is good about being different.

Michael introduced me to Spectrum's program director in the fall of 2010. Subsequently, my role at Spectrum began as an adult volunteer myself. In January 2012, after volunteering for about eighteen months, I began ethnographic fieldwork at Spectrum involving participant observation in the space and conducting life history interviews with the youths who frequented Spectrum. I was in my field site doing participant observation and interviews two to three nights a week for eight months starting in January 2012 and then continued to have a regular presence at

Spectrum through the fall of 2013. This work generated thirty-three life history interviews with young people, ranging in length from forty-five minutes to two-and-a-half hours (see the appendix, "Profile of Research Participants"), one group interview with two participants, and hundreds of hours of participant observation.

Qualitative research is a messy process fraught with ethical challenges. These challenges are magnified when one's research involves marginalized groups, like LGBTQ-identified people, who are also minors, a vulnerable population by human subjects research standards.[22] My research was further complicated by my lack of experience doing qualitative research involving human subjects, meaning that some of the weaknesses in my methodology only became visible long after I stepped out of the field. Therefore I aim to lend some transparency here to my methodological process, in particular when it comes to informed minor assent and informed consent.[23]

Although I was not seeking out minors exclusively, I did expect to encounter minors in my research and therefore wrote a human subjects research protocol that anticipated this possibility. Human research with children requires additional protections by human subjects research standards, requiring researchers to take particular care in their methodological approach to protect this population.[24] With the help of my university's institutional review board (IRB), I wrote a protocol that protected the privacy and confidentiality of participants in the following ways. First, in the case of all interviewees, consent (for adults) and assent (for minors) was to be verbal and not written. It was argued that written consent/assent would create a paper trail between myself and the participants, making them vulnerable to backlash for their participation in the study. Second, parental permission for participation was waived for minor participants because it could force minor participants to disclose information about themselves to their parents that would make them vulnerable—for example, that they identify as gay—and because of the transitory nature of my field sites, where a youth might be there one day but not return for several days, weeks, or months, if ever, making it very difficult to secure parental permission. Third, my recruitment script, which I used daily in my field sites, was intentionally vague in its language so as not to publicly implicate participants, and it required that I not disclose publicly who had or had not participated in an interview.

Finally, because there was no written consent/assent or parental permission, the protocol did not allow me to collect contact information or do follow-up interviews with any participants in the research study.

Interview participation was voluntary for Spectrum attendees, and the IRB restricted me to minors fifteen years and older. I offered participants a fifteen-dollar gift card to a grocery store as an incentive. I recruited interview participants in two ways: by directly approaching individuals with whom I had built rapport over time, and by making open announcements during check-in (a daily practice in which everyone present in the space would come together and introduce themselves).

Interviews began with questions about Spectrum, including how the youths found it, how long they had been coming, and what they did and did not like about it. I would then ask them to tell me about their lives growing up: who raised them, what their family structure was like, where they lived, if their parents or guardians worked, stayed home, practiced religion, and more. Finally, we discussed their experience with sex, including their most significant intimate and sexual relationships, the things that most influenced their sexuality, their access to sex education, and their safer sex practices. Even though the nature of my interview questions were quite personal and intimate, I found that participants were generally comfortable speaking with me and disclosed many personal details about their private lives. In some cases, the youths expressed surprise at the ease with which they could talk with me about things like their sexual desires and behaviors. I of course have no way of knowing what the participants held back, but common to our conversations were stories of childhood sexual experiences, specific sexual desires, preferred sexual conduct and partners, experiences with abuse, and anxieties and fears about sex.

Consent/assent for participant observation was another challenge I faced in my field site. Technically speaking, I was required by my university's IRB to get permission from human subjects whom I would be observing during the process of my data collection. Given the transitory nature of Spectrum visitors, asking for consent/assent from every person who entered to site would make the data collection nearly impossible. Therefore, I asked the IRB to waive consent/assent for participant observation during unstructured activities in the space, arguing that these kinds of activities during drop-in hours constituted public behavior. The public setup and structure of Spectrum is one in which folks are congregating together in one large room, most conversations are held in public, and activities are highly visible to youth and adults alike.

Alternately, for more structured activities like workshops or education programs, I created a process for obtaining verbal consent/assent. At the beginning of each session I would read the participant informed consent/assent guidelines to the group, make clear my intentions to observe the group, explain confidentiality, and explain that something they say or do may be quoted or described anonymously in my research. After I shared this information I would step away, and a staff member would circulate a sign-in sheet in which youth had the option to state if they would not like to be observed during the activity. If even one person objected, the staff member would let me know quietly and I would leave the group activity. In order to prevent coercion, the sign-in sheets were anonymous, the youth used a unique identifier that only they knew, and the paperwork was managed by the staff at Spectrum. Over the course of my research at Spectrum, it was relatively rare that anyone objected to my presence in structured activities. Although this is based simply on anecdotal evidence, it seems like the more I was known by the group's members, the more likely they were to consent/assent to me being there. The time I spent in the space hanging out with Spectrum youth was critical to the success of my research.

The details I have shared here should give the reader a sense of how complicated and difficult it can be to do sexualities-based social science research with minors, which helps to explain why there is so little of it. Although I did not realize it at the time, it was rather remarkable that I was able to get a research protocol of this kind passed through a university IRB. I was lucky to be working with an IRB that understood the importance of the research while not inflating the potential risk of harm to participants, which too often is the case. Also, the IRB was likely more comfortable approving my research protocol because of the written letters of support I had from the organizations I was working with. I might have had a much more difficult time getting permission to do this research in a public school setting, for example, where I would have access to a broader swath of young people but where the anxieties about minors and sexuality are heightened. The perceived risk of harm to minor participants in sexualities-based research means that too much of the research is done in settings like Spectrum, where staff and researchers are likely to have shared interests, which arguably limits the findings.

A Note on Language

I use "LGBTQ" as an umbrella term throughout the book, recognizing that it is impossibly inadequate to describe the youth I did research with but that for the sake of shared understanding it is the most widely recognized term to describe people who are not straight-identified or cis-identified. The word "transgender" is "an umbrella term for describing a range of gender-variant identities and communities."[25] In line with a particular trend among transgender people, scholars, and activists, I generally substitute "trans*" for transgender. The asterisk is a concise way to account for all of the different ways the term "trans-" can be deployed in referring to gender-related matters. When necessary to make a particular point, I use the term "genderqueer" to distinguish people whose gender expression or identity is genderqueer or gender non-binary from transbinary people.

As previously stated, I use "queer" both to describe a way of being in the world that opposes normal (sometimes intentionally, sometimes not) and to describe sexual conduct and behavior. For the purpose of the discussion within, I avoid the increasingly popular use of "queer" as an umbrella term to describe any and all LGBTQ-identified people on the grounds that it obfuscates the argument I try to make throughout: that not all people who are LGBTQ-identified are queer, nor is homosexuality a necessary component of queerness.

I refer distinctly to three different modes of understanding sexuality: desire, identity, and conduct or behavior. I use "desire" to refer to one's sexual orientations, fantasies, and attractions. "Identity" refers to the socially constructed names and labels individuals adopt to describe themselves and/or their sexuality—which may or may not be related to the gender of the persons they are attracted to—such as "straight," "gay," "lesbian," "bisexual," "pansexual," and "queer." "Conduct" and "behavior" are used to describe actual sexual and intimate acts that individuals engage in. While I understand these terms intersect with one another, I also see them as distinct and mutually exclusive.

The set of terms used to refer to people's sexualities and sexual and gender identities evolved while I was doing my research and continue to evolve as I write this manuscript. By way of example, in 2014, Facebook expanded its options for "gender"—a category considered in its user profiles to be "basic info" along with one's name, birthday, the gender of persons they are "interested in," and religious and political affiliations—from two (male/female) to fifty-one. Users can also create custom categories if they do not find a gender identity that appropriately describes them among the prepopulated choices. The point is that, at this very moment, language used to describe gender and sexuality is changing rapidly in U.S. society. Therefore, I use the language that is most likely to convey a mutual understanding between myself and the reader while trying to be most respectful toward the people whom I describe throughout.

Embracing Ambivalence

The dominant life-course narrative in U.S. culture is one in which becoming an adult means finding your self. This discourse is also prevalent in narratives about LGBTQ people becoming their "true" selves once they disclose their sexual and/or gender identities to others. Yet if we push back against the idea of adolescence being a hormone-crazed stopover between childhood and adulthood and instead embrace the notion that the process of becoming is as important as who we become, we can learn something from the youth of Spectrum.[26] Young people's often ambiguous sense of themselves as sexual, gendered persons is not a result of them not yet knowing who they are; it is who they are. Because young people today are exposed more to queer, homoerotic ways of being in the world, they are developing new ways to talk about themselves within the dominant sex/gender order, such as coining new terms like "pansexual" and "heteroflexible" to describe sexual attractions and orientations or by expanding gender pronouns beyond the binary. As this process develops, they expose the human propensity toward sexual and gender fluidity. Adolescent sexuality, in its queerness, requires language and identity formation that acknowledges the unfixed nature of our gender and sexuality.

There is a justifiable fear that if we let go of a bioessentialist understanding of sexual orientation—and increasingly gender identity, too—the rights-based gains that have been made to protect LGBTQ people will be overturned by the argument that one chooses to be gay and/or trans* and therefore does not deserve protection under constitutional law. It is not my intent to show that people choose to be gay in opposition to being straight; rather, I intend to show that all sexual and gender identities are sociohistorical formations.[27] I hope to demonstrate this through my interpretation and analysis of my experiences getting to know the youth of Spectrum.

Rather than take for granted that the youth of Spectrum *are* LGBTQ youth, *Growing Up Queer* is about how they have *become* sexual and gendered persons. My analysis shows how sexual orientation and gender identity are not simply something one has but are influenced by the various social contexts we occupy. Although we are living in a historical moment in which homoeroticism is more normalized than it has been for several generations, that doesn't mean that people are not still excluded, bullied, and segregated for being queer, so it is important to pay careful attention to what and who is queered in a contemporary context.

Chapter Overview

Chapter 1 places Spectrum into geographical, social, and political context for the reader. I explain where Spectrum is located, what it looks and feels like, and its role in relationship to contemporary LGBTQ youth centers and gay-straight alliances. I describe the differences in the U.S. political climate in which I did my fieldwork to the political climate in 2017–2018, as this book started its publication process; a lot has changed between 2010 and 2018. LGBTQ youth activism and spaces are a relatively new phenomenon that, I suggest, are influencing how young people across the sexual and gender spectrum understand themselves in society. In this chapter I challenge some of society's assumptions about risk and resilience among LGBTQ youth and help the reader to better understand Spectrum as a living, breathing, evolving space.

In chapter 2, I show how some young people become sexual by highlighting how gender non-conforming behavior and characteristics are used to explain how people know that they are gay. Heteronormativity acts as a straightening device, meaning that it's not enough to be heterosexually oriented; one must also be appropriately masculine and feminine to be straight. Further, heteronormativity is so entrenched in society that young people may interpret their violations of heterosexual scripts as necessary evidence that they are not straight. In these cases young people have adopted the binary sexual order in which they assume that, if they are teased for being too femme or too butch, or if they experience same-sex sexual fantasies and desires, then they must be gay, which tightens the restriction of binary gender and sexuality. Beyond genderqueerness and homoerotic desires, Spectrum youth have formed their queer identities based on their experiences with class, race, ability, nationality, and more, exposing the ways that heteronormative culture is not just straight but also white and middle class. Therefore, finding a place like Spectrum, which serves as a release valve from the pressures of heteronormativity, is often the first time these young people start to have a sense of belonging in society. Spectrum, then, is a place of socialization where young people experiencing a queer subjectivity learn the language and the culture of queer.

Chapter 3 examines how the youth of Spectrum are forming gender identities in the context of transgender phenomena, a paradigm shift in the way gender is represented, understood, and explained. By being a space where genderqueerness is accepted and embraced, Spectrum is a kind of queer utopia. At Spectrum young people are allowed to feel ambivalence about their gender and can play with pronouns, gender expression, and identity. For those queer young people whose gender expression and identity is ambiguous—meaning that what they look like challenges mainstream society's notions of what a boy or a girl is— Spectrum may be the first place they feel the liberation of not having to be one or the other. Spectrum youth are learning to complicate gender, be aware of the role gender attribution plays in our interactions with each other, and forge resistance to the entrenched gender binary.

Chapter 4 shows how important alternative media is to the formation of queer cultural scenarios that speak to the sexual subjectivities of the youth of Spectrum. While acknowledging that there are now far more representations of queerness in mainstream media, I challenge the assumption that mainstream media has handily embraced homoeroticism and genderqueerness. I show how queer media, like erotic fan fiction and *anime*, has an established history of providing alternatives to the heteronormative mainstream, alternatives that, thanks to the internet, are more and more accessible to young people from all walks of life. The youth of Spectrum, who were among the first generation of kids in the United States to be exposed to *anime* like *Sailor Moon* on network television, grew up on representations of queer sexualities and genders that were previously censored out of mainstream television. In this way, queer media that resist heteronormativity have the power to influence the sexual subjectivity and gender identity formation of young people. Therefore it's not that mainstream media are becoming less homophobic and shifting cultural norms in the United States. Rather, young people have access to so much more media outside the mainstream—including self-produced media like fan fiction—that influences their understanding of themselves and the world they live in. More than ever, diverse media, more so than family, school, and religion, are shaping how young people become sexual, gendered persons.

Acknowledging that the youth of Spectrum tend to disclose their sexual and gender identities to parents at a relatively young age, chapter 5 explores the role of family in the formation of these youths' sexualities and genders. It was often the case with Spectrum youth that, rather than rejection, they encountered loving support about their sexuality from their parents. But because the narrative of negative coming-out experiences with parents and family is so prevalent, even those youth who didn't have bad experiences considered themselves lucky or unusual. The youth of Spectrum are of a generation of kids who are the first to grow up in a society in which same-sex couples and genderqueer parents rearing children have become significantly socially acceptable. In addition to having queer parents, the youth of Spectrum were raised by queer siblings, cousins, aunties and uncles, grandparents, and other influential family members. I speculate that young people are sharing their queer sexual and gender identities with their parents at a younger age because of gender non-conformity that leads parents to make assumptions about their child's sexuality, because they are more frequently exposed to LGBTQ family members and loved ones, and because these particular parents do not conform to the white, middle-class, heteropatriarchal regime of the Standard North American Family. Queer family formation has broad implications not just for same-sex couples but for the way U.S. society understands and recognizes family in general.

Finally, I conclude with a discussion of the importance of broad-based coalitional organizing that moves beyond oversimplified identity politics. As society evolves away from binary understandings of sexuality and gender, identities that essentialize those binaries will become less and less useful. Further, by acknowledging that as LGBTQ becomes more normal the boundaries between normal and queer get redrawn, those of us who are concerned about the well-being of young people would be wise to pay close attention to how bodies are queered beyond simply sexuality and gender. I point to the Black Lives Matter and transgender movements as examples of twenty-first-century social justice movements that are responding to the ways that identity-based movements of the late twentieth century often failed to protect their most marginalized members.

1

Welcome to Spectrum

A Place to Be Queer

In seventh grade Brian, who is twenty-one years old, white, and queer-identified, began sharing with his parents that he was experiencing homosexual desires. His pediatrician recommended Spectrum to his mom when Brian expressed that he felt he needed more support than he was getting at home and at school. He told me, "I was just looking for support; I was looking for community. I was looking for people who were going through the same things I was going through and have the same feelings I have." So in eighth grade he made the plunge and attended Spectrum for the first time. His father came with him and hung out reading a newspaper while Brian made his way. I asked him if he remembered what it felt like that first day:

> Yes, I remember the first time I walked in. It was a Wednesday 'cause we looked up the schedule and they said there was a support group, and I was like oh, maybe I should go the next day at the support group for the first night. And my dad was like, "Well, why don't we [his parents] come the first day?" 'cause I'm from the suburbs. Never really ventured too much out, I never, before I started coming to Spectrum, I rarely came downtown. . . . It was the week right after queer prom, so everyone was kind of winding down from that and there was a lot of talk about oh, you know, "I did this at queer prom," and "I saw this person," and whatnot . . . but also at that time of the year they're also doing their annual survey, so I remember . . . my first day being overwhelmed a little bit, but then also getting this big [survey], and back then we didn't do it on computers, we did it on paper! And so I had this big packet, you know, full of survey to do, and I'm like well, "I'm really coming out," I had to fill out this survey and like identify myself and all that stuff, so, that was overwhelming at first too . . . just like, what is this place? I remember they were also talking

that there was a drag show that Friday, and so I went to the drag show and that was like, wow, like overwhelming. There was so many more youth. . . . It was interesting to see. I had never been to a drag show, I didn't even know what a drag show was.

Entering Spectrum for the first time is not for the faint of heart; it takes an incredible amount of courage and self-awareness to walk up to the building, enter the front doors, and find your way down to the youth space. Someone who is afraid to be associated with the LGBTQ community likely would not come anywhere near The Resource. A majority of the youth who make their way down the stairs and into the dazzling milieu that is Spectrum are likely to be well on their way to recognizing their gay, lesbian, bisexual, or queer sexuality and/or queer gender identity. They learn about Spectrum from peers, siblings, and—like Brian— often from adults in their lives. For many youths there, making their way into Spectrum also means "really coming out," as Brian described. Brian refers to the survey he was asked to fill out the first time he attended, which was part of data collection being conducted by a local university.[1] The survey asks youth many questions about the climate at their school, at home, and outside in the world, various health-related topics like tobacco, drug, and alcohol use, suicidal thoughts and other self-harming behaviors, religion, support systems, and demographics. Respondents are also asked to identify their gender and sexual identities and answer questions about sexual conduct. Once that initial survey is completed, youth are asked to fill out The Resource's census every time they come. They are asked their age, race/ethnicity, whether or not they are experiencing homelessness, health insurance status, citizen status, gender and sexual identity, and whether or not they get a free or reduced lunch at school. What does it mean to name your sexual orientation and gender identity? How do youth decide which terms best describe who they are? Do they maintain those identities once they have completed the survey, or do they feel free to change them? This process of completing a survey and census—one in the service of research, the other a mechanism for The Resource to justify its existence to funders—is part of young people's identity formation.

I share Brian's account of discovering Spectrum because it shows some of the processes of becoming that he encountered on his journey there. From the adults—his parents and his physician—who identified Spectrum as a resource, to the university-administered survey he was asked to complete on his first visit to the space, to the introduction to downtown and drag, two things he was previously unexposed to, Brian's formation of a sexual and gender identity is not simply a matter of experiencing desire. My hope is that these processes of how youths come to understand their sexualities and genders become visible throughout the book, helping us to think about how we all become sexual, gendered beings. Because Spectrum is so much a part of this process, I spend some time here putting it into regional, historical, and political context.

Where Spectrum Lives

Spectrum, and The Resource, the larger LGBTQ organization that houses the youth program, are located in the heart of a bustling urban community in the western United States that is home to industry leaders in health care, technology, and investment services and to over half a million people. In 2010, the city's skyline, a growing mass of skyscrapers and cranes, attested to the economic vibrancy of an economy seemingly untouched by the recent recession. The urban center boasts a busy public transportation system with buses and light rail; multiple professional sports stadiums and arenas; art, history, and science museums; and a booming dining and nightlife industry. Youth often arrive at Spectrum after having come from downtown, where young people are known to congregate in public spaces, shop at stores like Hot Topic or H&M, or see movies at the multiplex theater.

The Resource is located in a mixed-use residential community near downtown that has historically been known as this city's gay and lesbian neighborhood. Like many gayborhoods across the country, this slightly seedy yet creative and lively place is undergoing urban development and gentrification that is changing its look and feel.[2] In many ways, this neighborhood is losing its queerness. As a result of the new urbanization and creative economies movements, the hardscrabble businesses and residents who have so long given it a special charm have been pushed out to make room for a whiter, more educated, and straighter population. It is this same influx of development money that helped The

Resource to purchase and renovate a building on one of the busiest and most eccentric city thoroughfares.

The largest racial/ethnic minority in the city are Hispanics, who make up 32 percent of the population, followed by Blacks at 11 percent, Asians at 2.8 percent, and Native Americans at 1.3 percent. Whites make up more than 50 percent of the population, and residential racial segregation is the norm. It is one of the most educated cities in the United States, where 92 percent of the city's population has completed high school and 35 percent have bachelor's degrees. While the median family income is just under $40,000, with the median home price at $383,000, it has increasingly become the case that the wealthy are pushing the middle- and working-class residents out of the urban center and into its periphery. Regardless, this city remains one of the most racially and economically diverse communities in the state and bears the brunt of providing a disproportionate amount of social services to individuals and families in need.[3]

The Resource is one of the much-needed service providers in the city. Its mission is to serve all members of the LGBTQ community, yet the various programs and services it provides—including health services, legal aid, addiction services, and outreach—are often used by those who do not have the resources to access these services privately. The same can be said of The Resource's LGBTQ youth drop-in center Spectrum, where the bulk of the youth in regular attendance are from working-class and low-income backgrounds, many of whom are experiencing or have experienced homelessness, are struggling to complete or have dropped out of high school, and generally do not have the resources or support that many middle- and upper-class teenagers might have, including access to health insurance, quality education, and jobs. While white youth make up the majority of the Spectrum community numerically, youth of color—particularly Latinx and Black youth—are strongly represented in the space. The combination of sexual and gender minority youth from a wide range of race/ethnic and class identities results in an unusually diverse space for this typically segregated city.

Going Inside

Michael, who identifies as gay and is white, cismale, and barely in his forties, rolls up on his bike wearing a T-shirt, cargo shorts, and sneakers. He locks up and takes me inside Spectrum for my first visit. We walk up a small flight of concrete steps and through the glass double doors. Someone behind the reception desk, recognizing Michael, waves us in. The reception area is bright and clean, with that brand-new, not-quite-lived-in feeling, but I don't get a chance to see much of it as we take a hard right and enter a stairwell headed for the basement, where Spectrum is. At the bottom of the stairs is a small vestibule with colorful art hanging on the walls. The art is a project the kids at Spectrum worked on with a community art group, intended to represent youth participants' relationship to Spectrum and each other. It makes for a warm transition for visitors who exit the outside world and enter Spectrum.

After opening another door, we encounter a desk with a sign-in sheet and stacks of various pamphlets and flyers: Some announce events, some are public health flyers about sexually transmitted infections and suicide awareness. On the other side of the chest-high counter, a kid wearing all black with shoulder-length hair, dyed black with a blue streak, and multiple facial piercings greets us. Behind the L-shaped counter that separates the reception area from the rest of the space, I see a wall of lockers, a few computer stations for staff, and the soundboard for the PA system, which is currently plugged into someone's iPod. Loud pop music fills the room.

Michael leads me to the right, and we walk along the reception counter as the space opens up to a large room with couches, stuffed chairs, and benches surrounding a low-lying table. There are just a few kids hanging out here, lounging on the couches, faces buried in their smart phones. In the lounge area there is a big-screen television and a foosball table. As we continue around to the right, another large, open room becomes visible. In it are long, banquet-style tables and stacking chairs, the far wall lined with cabinets and a countertop. Along the edge of these open spaces are bookshelves filled with the books that make up Spectrum's lending library. Various doors leading to other rooms circle the space. There is a small room Michael explains is the "drag closet," where clothes, makeup, mirrors, and the like are kept for drag shows. Next to it is a small, private consultation space. The remaining rooms are private offices for the various staff. There are two gender neutral bathrooms and a kitchen with a fridge, freezer, sink, and microwave.

Much like upstairs, Spectrum feels brand spanking new. The furniture is new, the rug on the floor is new, the paint on the walls is new. It's a bit antiseptic and definitely unlived in. As he gives me the tour, Michael explains that the youth have been reluctant to make the switch to the new space. The old Spectrum, he tells me, was filled with ratty old couches, graffiti-covered walls, and an actual DJ booth, not just a PA behind a counter. Youth entered the space through a back door, so they didn't have to encounter any staff at The Resource if they didn't want to. Their refusal to show up seemed to be a bit of a protest to the relocation, although currently there is a contingent of kids posted up outside the building, smoking. The consensus among the adults is that the youth will reconsider coming inside once winter is on its way. For now, though, it is quiet and slow, adults often outnumbering youths in the space. During these early days at Spectrum, I often feel like I am hiding in plain sight. I hover behind the reception counter with the other adults and staff, reluctant to approach the kids quite yet. It will only be a matter of time, though, before I feel at home here.

Safe Spaces

From a generational perspective, LGBTQ-identified youth, gay-straight alliances (GSAs) in colleges and high schools, and drop-in centers like Spectrum are collectively a relatively new phenomenon. Of course, young people have always experienced homosexual desire and engaged in homosexual conduct, but it is within the context of the modern gay rights movement that people have adopted labels like "lesbian," "gay," "bisexual," and more as identities marking one's sexuality.[4] In fact, the gay and lesbian rights movement—unlike the race-based Civil Rights Movement and the feminist movement—was missing a large youth-led contingent during its early stages.[5] This was likely due both to the small number of self-identified gay and lesbian youth and the deeply stigmatizing and homophobic association of gay men with pedophilia.[6] The first inkling of a youth-based gay and lesbian rights movement occurred on college campuses in the 1970s where students were advocating for their right to access to higher education. It wasn't until almost twenty years later that similar student-rights-based arguments were made by high school students.[7]

While the growing number of gay-identified young people was resulting in a bona fide youth contingent of the gay rights social movement, a growing concern about the well-being of LGBTQ youth in the realm of public health, social work, and psychology was also developing. A 1989 U.S. Health and Human Services report on trends in youth suicide included a contribution from the San Francisco–based social worker Paul Gibson, who made a claim that there is a strong correlation between youth suicide and homosexuality.[8] While Gibson was just one of many experts working with youth who had come to recognize that sexual and gender minority youth were vulnerable, his particular claim—that gay teens are two to three times more likely to attempt suicide than their heterosexual peers—grew legs and has since become one of the most frequently cited "facts" used to argue that LGBTQ youth are at risk. Although Gibson's concerns about gay youth suicide are valid, the data are disputed for being inflated, and the report critiqued, for not being grounded in the scientific method, therefore there are many who doubt the number is as high as he claimed. To be fair, Gibson never claimed to be a scientific researcher; he was asked to write a statement for the report based on his extensive experience working with gay- and lesbian-identified homeless youth. Regardless, it has been argued that the now commonly cited "Gibson numbers" resulted in the widespread recognition of the *at-risk* LGBTQ youth subject.[9]

The point is not to deny that homophobic bullying and violence are real problems that result in negative outcomes for victims—like suicide—but the story of the Gibson numbers is important to understand in the context of the construction of an LGBTQ youth subject. The story of LGBTQ youth precarity—or its correlate, resilience—has become the dominant narrative, leaving little room for an understanding of queer youth in other ways.[10] And perhaps most significantly, the narrative of risk, which has situated academic scholarship on LGBTQ youth squarely in the fields of public health and psychology, has overshadowed the strength of the LGBTQ youth social movement. While this volume is not a book about social movements or organizations, it is important to recognize Spectrum's role in the context of being a youth drop-in center for what are now broadly considered to be at-risk youth. The rise of the GSA in schools and youth drop-in centers like Spectrum is arguably a result of the at-risk narrative that began with the Gibson numbers.

As the sociologist Melinda Miceli carefully documents in her book *Standing Out, Standing Together*, the rise of GSAs in high schools gained most of its traction during the 1990s, bolstered by the Health and Human Services report mentioned above. Gay-straight alliances are "groups established by students for the purpose of uniting with those who shared their interest in discussing gay rights issues, educating their school community about these issues and the extent and effect of homophobia in their school, and making school policy more supportive of LGBT students' rights."[11] Indeed, a meta-analysis of research that examined the existence of GSAs and youth self-reports of school-based victimization found that "GSA presence is associated with significantly lower levels of youth's self-reports of homophobic victimization, fear of safety, and hearing homophobic remarks," forms of abuse that result in students missing school, getting poor grades, and engaging in various self-harming behaviors.[12] Gay-straight alliances have come to be understood as an important component of creating safer schools for sexual- and gender- minority students. What is not clear about the findings that show that having a GSA in a school results in less homophobic bullying is the causation. It remains unclear whether the existence of a GSA in a school makes the school safer or if the culture of the school, one where a GSA is allowed to exist, means that it is less homophobic to begin with.[13]

According to the 2015 Gay, Lesbian, and Straight Education Network (GLSEN) School Climate Study, which surveyed over ten thousand sixth- to twelfth-grade students in schools in every state in the country, just over half of those surveyed have a GSA or similar club in their school. The GLSEN study also found that homophobic bullying is most prominent in rural/small-town locales in the South and Midwest regions of the United States.[14] Therefore it is possible that higher rates of homophobic bullying can be better explained by geography than by in-school resources, although certainly the two are interrelated. My research does not address the question about whether or not GSAs encourage tolerance or if tolerance encourages GSAs, but I want to provoke thoughtful interrogations of the role *place* plays in the formation of sexual and gender identities.

Compared to GSAs, less is known about the impact LGBTQ centers' youth programs have on kids. By the time I began my research in the second decade of the 2000s, LGBTQ centers were commonplace in cities and towns all over the country. When I checked the 2017 directory for CenterLink, a national organization of LGBTQ centers, it had 185 registered members.[15] According to CenterLink, almost every state in the United States has at least one center, and some states have many. There may be more, given that not every LGBTQ center in the country is a registered member of CenterLink. It is safe to assume that many of these centers have youth programming of some sort, although it's difficult to say exactly how many LGBTQ youth drop-in centers there are across the country. LGBTQ youth services come in a variety of forms, some well established within a community, others that are more grassroots in nature. To my knowledge, there does not exist a formal record of them.

There is little work in sociology that examines LGBTQ youth centers specifically. While there is a significant amount of research done in psychology, social work, and public health involving LGBTQ youth and LGBTQ youth centers, the focus tends to be on health and well-being outcomes. For example, in their study of a youth drop-in program for sexual and gender minority youth in Houston, published in *Health Promotion Practice*, health science researcher Kim Romijinders and her colleagues found that "secondary social ties were strengthened" for youth attending the program, resulting in reports of "increased confidence and self-esteem."[16] This study reinforces the at-risk/resilience narrative, as the research question is centered on mental health outcomes for youth who attend this program.

An exception can be found in a cultural anthropology study published in the early 1990s. One of the first known gay youth support groups started in 1979 at Horizons, a LGBTQ community center in Chicago, later documented by Gilbert Herdt and Andrew Boxer in their ethnography *Children of Horizons: How Gay and Lesbian Teens Are Leading a Way Out of the Closet*.[17] Herdt and Boxer's ethnography set out to make LGBTQ youth visible and seems to be one of the first academic works to point to the power and promise of LGBTQ youth. But *Children of Horizons*, like the article mentioned previously, operates from the perspective of LGBTQ youth as a given, rather than LGBTQ spaces as places where identities are formed. In her review of the book in 1994, the sociologist Nancy Whittier makes note of this lack: "Also striking [about *Children of Horizons*] is an essentialist view of sexual identity. Despite their focus on shifting definitions of what it means to be gay or lesbian, Herdt and Boxer leave the social construction of same-sex desire unexamined. The assertion that youth are confused not about their sexual identity but about how to act on it aims to defuse accusations that adults 'socialize' youth to be gay or lesbian. Yet this assumption makes it impossible to examine how youths construct and interpret same-sex desire."[18] Whittier's concern can be applied to all of the ways society takes for granted that the LGBTQ youth is a recognizable subject. While it may be true these youth-focused resources like GSAs and LGBTQ youth centers provide much needed support for a previously hidden and isolated population, the fact of their existence has the effect of influencing how young people understand their sexual and gendered selves and, in some ways, may "leave the social construction of same-sex desire unexamined." What follows is a reflection on the effects of shifting ideologies within Spectrum.

Becoming Sexual Now

One brisk January afternoon, Michael and I stepped out of Spectrum to grab a coffee. We chatted about my research project while walking down the street together. Always supportive of me, he expressed his excitement about the work and asked, "Are you going to talk about the influence the adult staff of Spectrum have on the youth in the space?" He explained that Sid and César, two adult staff at Spectrum, are both politically progressive and that the projects and discussions that happen in Spectrum often revolve around progressive politics. Having been an adult volunteer at Spectrum for a decade, Michael has experience with many iterations of staff, and not all of them have been what he described as "political"; he says some "were just concerned with keeping the youth out of jail." His point was not that one approach—ideological compared to practical—is better than another but, rather, that the goals of the adult staff set the tenor of the Spectrum experience. I am not sure how to answer his question, namely because my role as an ethnographer is to observe and analyze what I see and experience, which will be limited to the Spectrum of right now. Yet I would come to understand over time how important his question is to the findings I share in this book.

Throughout this volume, I show how Spectrum youth come to form their identities as sexual and gendered persons, and I make a case that they be understood as queer-oriented. And while I don't think it's the case that their queer orientation is a result of the ideologies of the adult staff of Spectrum, it is true that the staff's ideologies inform how the youths interpret their experiences. Further, it is equally important to acknowledge how the youths themselves are agents of change, whose influence will also leave its mark. As the youths encounter particular ideologies or ways of framing sexuality and gender at Spectrum—in this case, framings that are informed by a particular progressive politics— they may adopt similar framings, but in an adaptive way that suits the reality in which they live. The philosopher of science Ian Hacking, in his discussion of how scientific inquiry classifies people, suggests there is a looping effect in which efforts at classifying people create "moving targets because our investigations interact with them, and change them. And since they are changed, they are not quite the same kind of people as before."[19] While Hacking is particularly interested in the looping effects created by scientific inquiry, this can also be applied to how we understand identity formations around sexuality and gender. The youth of Spectrum are entering adolescence in a particular historical moment in which LGBTQ subjectivities are normalized, compared to previous generations. By thinking about the role Spectrum—and various other agents of socialization—play in the youths' processes of forming sexualities and genders, we can ask ourselves, What is different about becoming sexual now?

Political Backlash

During the time I spent at Spectrum, the United States was in the midst of a paradigm shift in terms of LGBTQ rights and awareness. Over the course of the three years I was doing research there, the U.S. military's "Don't Ask, Don't Tell" policy and the Clinton-era Defense of Marriage Act (DOMA) were both repealed.[20] For the first time, a sitting U.S. president expressed public support for gay marriage.[21] The "It Gets Better" campaign exploded in response to LGBTQ bullying.[22] An increasing number of high-profile individuals came out publicly as lesbian, gay, or bisexual, including MSNBC news anchor Anderson Cooper and Los Angeles Galaxy soccer player Robbie Rogers. History was made during the 2012 election when three states—Maine, Maryland, and Washington State—passed voter-approved same-sex marriage laws and Wisconsin elected the first openly gay U.S. senator, Tammy Baldwin.[23] Further, awareness of trans* rights increased steadily. Feature stories on trans* children ran in major national newspapers like the *New York Times* and the *Washington Post*.[24] Finally, the 113th U.S. Congress passed a version of the Employment Non-Discrimination Act (ENDA) that for the first time included gender identity as a protected status.[25] It is important to remember that this era was the context for my field research because so much has happened since I stepped out of the field after the summer of 2013.

Probably the two most significant changes to occur immediately following the completion of my research would be the 2015 Supreme Court decision in *Obergefell v. Hodges*, which guaranteed the right to marry for same-sex couples, and the skyrocketing increase in awareness of trans* rights. While often centered around celebrity trans activists like Laverne Cox, a transwoman actor best known for her role on the television show *Orange Is the New Black*, and Caitlyn Jenner, the U.S. Olympian and athlete who came out publicly as a transwoman in 2015, trans* experience has also been echoed throughout the country in the lives of many everyday people. Countless stories about trans* children continue to surface in various media outlets.

While I was doing my fieldwork at Spectrum from 2010 to 2013, observing what appeared to be a powerful progressive moment in LGBTQ rights, a sea change was occurring that would result in a Republican sweep of the 2016 elections and which threatens to reverse many of the gains made by the LGBTQ movement. Even though this book demonstrates evidence of progress through the narratives of Spectrum youth, I have been cautiously optimistic about what that means for the future of sexuality and gender in this country. Prior to the 2016 elections, I felt that the country was clearly moving in the direction of more and more acceptance (not just tolerance) of same-sex sexuality and gender fluidity, but that queerness would always be a marker of exclusion for some. But the Republican wins in 2016 shook me to my core, leaving me filled with cynicism and doubt about the country's ability to move past old-fashioned, bigoted norms regarding sexuality.

In what appears to be a backlash to progress, as I completed this book manuscript in 2017, the Republican Party gained control of the White House, the House of Representatives, and the Senate. The president appointed one U.S. Supreme Court justice, Neil Gorsuch, a politically conservative originalist, and will likely have the opportunity to appoint another.[26] President Trump also appointed Jeff Sessions as U.S. attorney general—who as a former Alabama attorney general and U.S. senator for the state of Alabama consistently opposed various LGBTQ rights measures.[27] As so-called "bathroom bills" that resemble legalized segregation of trans* people are popping up in states all over the country, the Trump administration is rescinding the Department of Education's trans*-friendly interpretation of Title IX as a law that prohibits gender discrimination along with sex discrimination in federally funded educational institutions.[28] Conflating a budget-related debate over covering medical services for those serving in the military and suffering symptoms of gender dysphoria with all transgender people, in July 2017 President Trump tweeted his intentions to ban all transgender people from serving in the military.[29] And finally, the Southern Poverty Law Center reported an increase in hate groups across the country, including those who express bigotry toward LGBTQ people.[30]

While the state of California amended its education code with the passage of the California Healthy Youth Act in October 2015, mandating the most comprehensive, LGBTQ inclusive and affirming sex education policy in the country, in 2017 the Trump administration and the Republican Party are threatening to revive abstinence-only policies from the days of the George W. Bush administration, policies that the Obama administration had been consistently defunding since 2009.[31] It has become painfully clear that the United States is deeply divided by partisan political values when it comes to rights-based policies regarding sexuality and gender. While surely an oversimplification, those divisions appear to be geographical: The Midwest and the South along with suburban and rural communities seem to be in opposition to the West Coast and Northeast and large metropolitan enclaves.[32] In the wake of the 2016 presidential election there has been much talk about how the Republican presidential campaign played on race-, class-, and nationality-based anxieties and fears that helped to mobilize white voters across class for Donald Trump. Support for Trump is also evidence of a negative response to LGBTQ gains, inherent in the critiques of political correctness among so-called elites.[33]

Therefore any analysis of queer youth experience in the contemporary United States must be geographically situated: Around the same time that the state of California was amending its education code in the name of protecting children, the state of North Carolina passed House Bill 2, the Public Facilities Privacy and Security Act, one of the most transphobic pieces of legislation in the country, also in the name of protecting children.[34] The Spectrum experience described within these pages might be seen by some as a metronormative one that "reveals the rural to be the devalued term in the urban/rural binary governing the spatialization of modern U.S. sexual identities."[35] But to suggest that Spectrum is progressive because of its metropolitan setting is not meant to also suggest that suburban, ex-urban, and rural settings are regressive.[36] Rather, it indicates a deep political divide within the United States that is playing out along racialized, classed, gendered, and sexualized lines. It remains unclear whether or not the United States, on the whole, is becoming less trans- and homophobic or not; what is clear is that the nation is divided over the significance of identities to experiences and how exactly to solve the problems related to inequality that plague the nation.

Yet there is something else at work here that complicates a simple urban versus rural moral divide. I am struck by the presence of young, gay white men in the so-called alt-right movement: men like Milo Yiannopoulos and Lucian Wintrich, who are not rural conservatives but high-profile media pundits who live and work in major urban centers like London, Washington, DC, and New York.[37]

Milo Yiannopoulos is a British political commentator and former editor of the "alt-right" media outlet Breitbart News, who is perhaps most infamous for the February 1, 2017, University of California Berkeley stop on his "Dangerous Faggot" speaking tour. His appearance on campus was the target of protests that resulted in a full-scale riot and cancellation of the event, sparking nationwide debates about free speech on college campuses. The English journalist and feminist activist Laurie Penny describes Yiannopoulos as "a bratty, vicious court jester of the new right who made a name for himself by saying grotesque and shocking things that he may or may not have ever believed. He does this compulsively, with no respect for the repercussions, or for the fact that a lot of people *do* believe what he says and act accordingly."[38]

According to a *New Yorker* profile written by contributing editor Andrew Marantz, Lucien Wintrich has no training as a journalist, but as a high-profile Trump supporter he announced at the New York City DeploraBall, a pre-inauguration celebration of Trump's election, "We've been in contact with people in the new Administration, and . . . I'm going to be . . . the youngest, gayest correspondent in the White House in history!"[39] In his profile, Marantz describes photos hanging on the walls of Wintrich's apartment of semi-clothed young men in "Make America Great Again" hats. Wintrich produced these photos for a series titled "Twinks 4 Trump."

These unapologetically gay members of the extreme right have made it their mission to denigrate the "libtards" whom they see as enemies of democracy. That the white male backlash includes a hefty representation of gay men supports arguments about normalization: that gayness—in and of itself—has become an acceptable way to be in U.S. society, as long as it is white, male, and heteronormative. As a high-profile conservative commentator, Yiannopoulos's obnoxious, bigoted behavior was willfully ignored—and sometimes embraced—by the Republican Party and the conservative Right in the United States until he was toppled from his pedestal by a very queer claim: He joked about his sexual experiences as a minor with a Catholic priest, suggesting that intergenerational sex among men was not always harmful. It was this—not his bigotry—that caused the Right to disavow him (and for book publishers Simon & Schuster to revoke the $250,000 advance they had offered him for his biography).[40]

To suggest that an LGBTQ-identified person represents a particular set of (progressive) goals or strategies is ridiculous. Yet too often that assumption is made. Perhaps ironically, when one can be both gay and profoundly vitriolic toward all kinds of marginalized people, it is a sign of the democratization of sexuality. It's also a sign that sexuality and gender are always constituted in relation to other identities like race, class, ability, and more. That characters like Yiannopoulos and Wintrich exist and are revered is less a sign that gayness has arrived than a sign that white supremacy and hegemonic masculinity persist.

The rights of LGBTQ-identified and queer people are not, by any stretch of the imagination, the sole target of the Trump administration. But there is no denying the profound social change that has occurred related to issues of sexuality and gender in the United States in the last fifty years. Young people, like those I met at Spectrum, are transforming the way we as a society think about sexuality and gender faster than people like myself can publish scholarship on the topic. Similarly, the political climate has shifted in ways I never could have anticipated since I stepped out of the field in 2013. Keeping these things in mind, I invite the reader to join me as I explore an LGBTQ youth drop-in center at a particular historical moment during the early stages of the twenty-first century.

2

"That Makes Me Gay"

Not Born That Way

I'm sitting across from Alex in stuffed chairs we've rolled into the consultation room at Spectrum for our interview. During my time at Spectrum, this space was mostly a storage room and my private interview space. Alex, nineteen years old, is a clean-cut white kid with blond hair and blue eyes. He wears his hair short and spiked and is typically in pressed jeans and a long-sleeved T-shirt with sneakers. He exudes a hyper energy and talks a million miles a minute. Alex is relatively new to Spectrum, but has been coming several times a week for a few months. Today is the first time I've seen him in a while, though, because he was away on a cruise with his family. I've not heard any Spectrum youth talk about going on a luxury vacation. This, and that he has his own car, certainly marks him as a class-privileged kid. Alex only came out as gay a little more than a year ago and he's still trying to learn the ropes, so to speak. He describes himself as a virgin and has never been in an intimate relationship with a man. During our interview I asked him, "When did you know what gay was? How did you figure that out?" He replied:

> I [was] probably like thirteen. And . . . it was just more like, my family would . . . once in awhile—they weren't big on it—but they'd say like, "He's so gay" or "He's a faggot." Stuff like that. And like, all the time that I was agreeing . . . I was the agree-er—but I actually asked, I was like, "What's gay?" Finally I asked [my brother], "What do you mean?" He's all . . . "It's this nasty guy who sleeps with another guy." That's all he said. . . . And I'm like, Oh my god. Okay. And I wanted to dig more. So I was like, "Well, what's wrong with it?" And he was like, "Well, I don't know, they're just attracted to the same sex." And I was like, Oh shit, that's me . . . a male that is attracted to a male. And I was like, Oh god, I look at males more than I do girls. That makes me gay.

Is it the case that a boy who "looks at" boys more than girls is therefore gay? I learned by talking with Alex that he retroactively pinpointed his understanding of himself as gay to a handful of interactions throughout his late childhood and adolescence where he recognized that when it came to characters on TV shows, pop stars, and in some cases, sneaking peaks at pornography, he found himself to be more interested in males than females. And although Alex learned that to call someone gay or a faggot was an insult of sorts, he did not actually know what "gay" meant. He had to ask his brother—who, in his infinite wisdom, shared that being gay was "nasty" but couldn't really explain why. By the time Alex and I met, he was most certainly interested in dating men but had not yet had the opportunity, and while he never had sex with them, he had dated girls before. For Alex, who by all accounts is a masculine, white, class-privileged, able-bodied young man, being gay meant having sexual desire for other men, and he learned the very clear message from his family that it was not okay to be gay.

Heteronormativity as a Straightening Device

The social theorist Michael Warner, editor of the 1993 essay collection *Fear of a Queer Planet*, uses the term "heteronormativity" to describe "culture's assurance [*read*: insistence] that humanity and heterosexuality are synonymous."[1] His point is that, as long as heterosexuality and the male/female gender binary are understood as ahistorical, fixed characteristics of humanity, anyone who does not conform to that norm is seen as less than human. Alex's brother cannot articulate why same-sex sexual desire is wrong, just that he knows it is wrong. The act of describing to his little brother that a man having sex with another man is "nasty" functions as a straightening device, or how Sara Ahmed describes heteronormativity:

> Think of tracing paper. Its lines disappear when they are aligned with the lines of the paper that has been traced: you simply see one set of lines. If all lines are traces of other lines, then this alignment depends on straightening devices, which keep things in line, in part by holding things in place. Lines disappear through such alignments, so when things come out of line with each other the effect is "wonky." In other words, for things

to line up, queer or wonky moments are corrected. We could describe heteronormativity as a straightening device, which rereads the "slant" of queer desire.[2]

Heteronormativity keeps the straight body in line. While Alex, at quite a young age, experienced an orientation of desire toward men, the heteronormative policing he encountered—in the exchange with his brother, for example—worked to straighten him out. In this case, it straightened him out enough that he learned to keep his desires to himself and to try to resist them until he was twenty years old. While, as I've explained, this book is about queer-oriented young people, it also illuminates the process of straightening that dominates social norms.

Spectrum Youth's Queer Orientation

I often asked interviewees to explain to me what their sexual identity means to them. As with Alex above, I wanted to know, how did he come to understand himself as gay? In this chapter, rather than try to explain the origin of same-sex desire or homosexuality, using the experiences shared with me by Spectrum youth, I show the various ways that these young people came to adopt their various sexual identities.

The accounts here show how the adoption of a sexual identity is a very pragmatic process that often has little to do with one's actual sexual behavior. Among their generation, homosexuality—as sexual conduct—is less and less stigmatized, as long as it resembles heteronormative expectations of sexuality and gender. For the youth of Spectrum, it is a "spatially and temporally" queer assemblage, and not simply their sexual orientation toward particular gendered bodies, that defines who they are.[3] All of us make meaning of our sexual selves within the context of a patriarchal, heteronormative structural system, in which symbols of masculinity and homophobia, which reiterate the normalcy of heterosexuality, inform identity development. Because Spectrum youth are socially outside the norm, owing to the various marginalized identities they occupy, they are queerly oriented and often excluded from the heteronormative mainstream. The youth of Spectrum are made queer by a straight society. Ahmed states that "queer unfolds from specific points from the life-world of those who do not or cannot inhabit the contours of heterosexual space. After all, some of us, more than others, look wonky."[4] The discussion that follows will show how some youth come to understand themselves as LGBTQ because of the way their conduct violates heterosexual scripts or because of their genderqueerness, while others come to their queer identities in the context of oppressive sexed, raced, gendered, and classed regimes, and finally how identities are formed as a result of discovering and becoming part of a community that validates one's way of being in the world.

Going Off Script

Some youths, when I asked them how they knew they were gay (or otherwise), recounted stories of looking at media as kids and being more interested in people of the same sex as themselves. For example, Alex told me that he did not like himself when he was younger. When I asked him why, he told me this story:

> I always knew there was something different about me. . . . I'm not a weirdo—but when I was younger . . . say we were watching *Power Rangers*, they [his brother and cousins] would always be checking out the girls, and I would be like, "Oh, look at the guys." Like Britney Spears, I was like, I love her music, she's pretty, but I love her music more. So I mean I always knew something was different, but I was ashamed kind of?

Fiona, whom I only met once, is a nineteen-year-old woman with creamy white skin, blond hair pulled back into a ponytail, and smiling eyes. Dressed in a loose-fitting flower-print tank top, jeans, and sandals, she sat down with me for an interview one hot summer day. She told me the story of how she got lost trying to find Spectrum the first time she came about a year ago. She had to call her dad for help, at which time he disclosed to her that he knew just where The Resource was because, as a pansexual person, he had been there himself! Fiona also identifies as pansexual now but considered herself straight until she was about sixteen, when she adopted a bisexual identity. When I asked her how she knew she was straight or bisexual, she said, "I don't think I ever knew I was straight because . . . you know how when you're young—you're a little kid—and you're like, I'm gonna look at porn? . . . I always looked at the women. Always." Although at first glance it is not surprising that as gay and pansexual-oriented youths, Alex and Fiona, respectively, disclosed that they found members of their gender more attractive than members of another gender, my point is not to examine the origin of their gendered desires. Rather, I am curious about the ways that they learned their gendered desires had a name.

Brian is a self-described "effeminate male" with a mischievous smile. He is warm and friendly and goes out of his way to make others feel at home at Spectrum. He describes himself as having "a bit of both genders of the binary inside." Although he is "biologically male" and somewhat awkward in the day-to-day, he transforms into a confident woman for Friday night drag shows. An activist invested in social justice, he is twenty-one years old, white, and queer identified. He came out to his parents and started coming to Spectrum when he was in seventh grade, which makes him one of the longest-attending Spectrum youths I spoke with. As a peer-staff member, Brian was welcoming to me from the start, and we have a comfortable, friendly relationship with each other. Similar to Alex's and Fiona's experiences described above, Brian shared that he had an early interest in the male body and would sketch nudes of men in a notebook. In the following example, he describes how his behavior with his first girlfriend, whom he was dating when he came out, did not conform to gendered expectations and therefore became one of the clues to his understanding of himself as queer:

> We were like, cuddling on the couch in my basement and I remember her being the one, kind of . . . you know, little spoon, big spoon? She was the big spoon of the cuddle kind of. And then she kind of said, "You know, actually, you're supposed to be like, have your arm around me and whatnot." And I'm like, "Oh, ok, like . . . that felt more comfortable like, your being the more, you know, dominant one." So, I think that was another wake-up call for me, you know?

Brian described being aware of how his feelings of desire and expressions of intimacy did not fit society's expectations, therefore internalizing a sense of being different or of somehow doing it wrong when comparing his behavior or feelings with that of friends or siblings. Yet again, what is interesting to me is how his girlfriend came to understand that being the "little spoon" was gendered female.

Heteronormative sexual scripts reinforce the logic of the sexual order. John Gagnon and William Simon's theory of sexual scripts is useful here. Sexual scripting theory shows how individuals employ a prescribed set of behaviors (scripts) in their interactions with others, which help people to understand when an interaction is sexual or not. These scripts are learned and socially influenced. These sexual scripts are how we differentiate between an intimate sexual encounter with a romantic partner and an intimate medical encounter with a doctor, for example, whereby the former should elicit feelings of arousal and desire and the latter should not.[5] Heteronormative sexual scripts reinforce dominant ideas about sexuality, in which the only acceptable sexual behavior, desires, or feelings occur between members of another, not the same, sex. The young people whose experiences are detailed here are responding to the dominant sexual order as they associate non-normative gender expression and/or violation of heterosexual scripts with proof of their gayness.

Genderqueerness and Sexuality

Although it is true that more people are identifying as LGBTQ at a younger age, it is not the case that *all* LGBTQ people adopt this identity earlier than before.[6] Coming out at an earlier age is tied to queerness, in particular, genderqueerness.[7] In the case of the youth discussed here, identifying as LGBTQ is more often tied to their genderqueer behavior as children and less about a strong innate sexual orientation or same-sex sexual behaviors. In addition, previously unrecognized and/or stigmatized options of various sexual and gender identities are now available to young people, allowing them to understand themselves as LGBTQ sooner in their lives. Many genderqueer young people, because of society's stubborn conflation of gender with sexuality, may even be prodded or pushed towards a sexual minority identity by parents, peers, teachers, and more, who assume their gender non-conformity to be a marker of their sexuality.

Miguel, a Mexican immigrant who is twenty years old and identifies as a gay man, has only recently started coming to Spectrum. His frame is small—he's shorter than me—and he is light skinned. Today he is wear-ing plaid shorts, an aqua blue polo shirt, and slip-on skate shoes. He wears his hair short and neat. Miguel speaks with his whole body, raising his arms and hands over his head, sitting up with one leg folded under-neath him. At one point during our interview he became particularly animated as he stood up and walked around the small room. He wears a silver chain around his neck, which he yanks down on and tosses back behind his shoulders as he speaks. Miguel has an exuberant, warm per-sonality, which he expresses by frequently reaching out and touching my hands or legs as he tells me his story. He came out to his friends and father in high school, but he says he always knew there was something different about him. Miguel's adoption of a gay identity happened in the United States in the context of an urban high school, but the following description is from his childhood in Mexico, where he was marked as a young boy for not being appropriately masculine:

> My voice was really . . . high pitched. I did sound like a girl. But that doesn't mean they had to give me, they used to label me, "Oh you little girl, you little this." Name calling. Being beaten you know, because maybe the sound of my voice didn't go with my boy body, you know? And maybe that's why I got picked on.

Jamil wears a long-sleeved hooded T-shirt he made himself in fash-ion class. The fabric is black with rainbow colored pinstripes, and there is a pocket for his hands sewn onto the front. Jamil loves music and dreams of being a pop star someday. He is outgoing and friendly, always smiling, revealing a small gap between his teeth. His hair is dark with a vestige of a bleached blond streak at his brow. A dark-brown-skinned, multiracial boy who is seventeen years old, he identifies his sexuality as open or bisexual and had been coming to Spectrum for about nine months at the time of his interview. He was cautious at the beginning of his interview. The verbal assent form I review with each interviewee in-cludes language warning the youth to not talk about illegal activity and suggests that talking about the past can sometimes trigger trauma. I feel that sometimes, after going over the assent, youth participants wonder what they have gotten themselves into, and Jamil appeared particularly overwhelmed at first. But once we started talking he relaxed and shared many details with me about a complicated childhood that involved some quite serious traumatic events involving the adults in his life. Generally speaking, though, Jamil has a loving family and is a happy-go-lucky person. He began identifying as bisexual in middle school. Like Miguel, he also experienced policing of his gendered behavior from his young uncles who pressured him to participate in masculine activities like football, which, he says, "wasn't ever my thing." He was also teased and bullied in elementary and middle school by peers for not conforming to a typical masculine gender:

> I went through a lot as a kid. I was struggling with . . . depression; I was facing bullying, and . . . being tormented for being the weird kid basically all the time. . . . Elementary school . . . no, middle school was worse. There were some days where people would be nice to me, but there'd always be that kid that would always be, "Oh, you're fruity and blah, blah, blah, and your voice is really high and blah, blah, blah . . ."

The previous examples show how these boys embody traits that go against gender norms, like having a high-pitched voice or by "acting fruity." The youths made meaning of the gender and queer policing they experienced by describing them as the characteristics that make them gay or bisexual.

Although it was predominantly among boys that I found gender non-conformance to be a signifier of sexuality, when I asked Zia, who is nineteen, Black, and identifies as queer, if her grandma—her primary caregiver—knows about her sexuality and that she hangs out at Spectrum she said, "When I told her, she just kind of knew . . . 'cause I'm butch as fuck [*laughs*]."

Heteronormativity is reinforced by gender norms—what we understand to be appropriately masculine or feminine. For example, rigid boundaries around femininity and masculinity, like the difference between a feminine- and a masculine-sounding voice, are used to shore up the logic of the sexual order. Others often label persons who violate those rigid gender norms, like men with lilting voices or women construction workers, as sexually deviant; violation of gender norms becomes a (faulty) tool used to predict another's sexual orientation or identity. So even as heterosexuality is becoming less compulsory, for the young people of Spectrum, the case remains that simply failing to demonstrate normative gender is enough to have one's sexuality called into question.[8] Sexuality is so seamlessly attached to gender and buoyed by heteronormativity that those who come off as genderqueer in behavior, appearance, or affect are quickly policed by family and peers for being *sexually* deviant.

This is important because ostensibly there are many gay, lesbian, and bisexual (LGB) individuals who do not share this childhood narrative of difference simply because nothing about their affect or behavior led others to question their sexuality. In fact, many people who adopt an LGB identity as adults may not have questioned their own heterosexuality as young people at all, far less had it questioned by others. Yet at the same time, some people who are teased and bullied as children for being queer remain heterosexually oriented throughout their lives. By the time these young people are telling me their story, they are already claiming a gay, bisexual, or queer identity. Thus, when asked to look back on their childhood and consider when they first realized they were gay, many of them identify this gendered difference as being a logical explanation for their gayness.

Surely many, many people experience feelings of desire for, and/or engage in sexual conduct with, members of their same gender. Similarly, many individuals who come off to others as genderqueer or violate heterosexual scripts never experience same-sex desire or sexual conduct. Therefore, neither of these things—same-gender desire nor queer gender—is what makes a person gay. In her book *Not Gay*, Jane Ward gives several examples of times and places where straight-identified men engage in homosexual behavior, while never wavering in their self-understanding of being straight. Ward explains it is precisely these men's unfailing belief in their innate sexual orientation that results in them never attaching gay meaning to their experiences with same-sex sexuality.[9] For Alex, Fiona, and Brian, something similar happens: The fact of their same-sex desire is the explanation for their gay, pansexual, or queer identity. Desire and behavior are not in and of themselves gayness; being gay or straight is a socially constructed process of identity formation. A process of straightening—social pressure to understand one's desires through the lens of the dominant norm—creates queer subjects. In the next section, I explore the intersections of sexuality, gender, race, and class.

Renaming Sexuality and Gender

Travon, a sixteen-year-old boy who has a white mother and a Black father, is an intellectually inquisitive kid with caramel-colored skin and short, curly hair. In his jeans, plain T-shirt, and clean sneakers, he showed no allegiance to any particular scene or subculture. A bright intellectual, Travon appeared relaxed during our interview. Although he didn't often meet my eyes, instead looking off to the side as he spoke, every once in a while, when he really wanted to get my attention, he'd look me straight in the eye and hold my gaze. Charming in his bashfulness, he seemed relatively comfortable talking with an adult, perhaps owing to his mother, with whom he has "hours-long conversations" with about politics, education, and religion. He explained how he had begun to consider ideas about gender fluidity and queerness, ideas that suggest sexuality and gender exist on a continuum rather than being fixed categories and that they can change over time. When I asked Travon how he sexually identifies, he answered that he identifies as queer:

> I did actually do it for a couple of different reasons. . . . I was in the time of my life. . . . When I originally came out I was bi, I came out only as bi. And then I realized I like guys better so I said I was gay. And then I started having reoccurring feelings for women so I went back to being bi and I was like, this is too much work, I identify as queer, it covers it all and it also doesn't exclude people like trans people and stuff and . . . I felt that it was a lot cooler to include everybody cause I'm not trying to build walls, like, if I like you then I'm going like you.

Travon's struggle to find an identity that suits him is difficult when the only options are gay, straight, or bi. His experience of his sexuality is that it's not fixed in such a way as to make those choices obvious. The young people at Spectrum seem to be aware of the fact that naming your sexuality based on the gender of the person you are attracted to doesn't always make a lot of sense.

A majority of the youths I interviewed identify their sexuality using widely recognized terms signifying the gender of the persons they are sexually attracted to, terms like "gay," "lesbian," and "bisexual." But this generation of youth have proliferated the number of sexual identity terms and now include identities like "pansexual" and "omnisexual" that describe one's sexual identity beyond the confines of gender. These terms acknowledge that sexual desire based on gender is a limited way to frame sexuality; one can be attracted to a variety of people for a variety of reasons. Some of the youths identify as queer, which quite intentionally distances identity from sexuality and/or gender exclusively and instead frames one's overall identity in opposition to the normal. In particular, a queer identity is often used by youth as a way to distance themselves from what they perceived to be a white, middle-class LGBTQ identity.

Ernie, whom I first introduced explaining the difference between gay and queer, is a twenty-one-year-old "queer-identified Chicano." Ernie says others often think his race is a "Black mix." His skin is reddish brown, and he keeps his dark, wavy hair cropped close to his head. Ernie is a sophomore at a state college nearby, is a leader in the youth community as an anti-racist and immigrant and queer rights activist, and is a longtime Spectrum regular. Ernie's moods are tempestuous, swinging from reflective to boisterous. As he explains what being queer means, he also talks about his race and class as being important to him:

> I like to call myself queer just 'cause it's . . . more like, fluid, like, it's very fluid. . . . You're not set to a standard or anything. . . . I dunno . . . people wanna be like "oh you're bisexual" but it's not, it's like past that, it's like, another level. . . . It's more fluid still. . . . I would date a girl, or a woman-identified person . . . and I've dated a man, like it just, that wouldn't matter to me. So that's one part of it and then just like also being a person of color and then also somebody who's like poor, and just stuff like that.

Ernie expresses a queer-of-color perspective, in that his sexuality is not the only thing that makes him queer. As the sociologist Roderick Ferguson has shown, "Black subjects in general, and working-class black subjects in particular [are] racialized as pathologically nonheteronormative."[10] Racial dynamics complicate homonormativity by blocking gay people of color from access to mainstream gayness. Combined with other marginalized identities, such as class, body size, ability, and nationality, the youth of Spectrum reveal that the more outside the white, middle-class norm you are, the more queer you are.

When Ernie first started coming to Spectrum three years ago, he says, "I couldn't identify with anybody else . . . mainly everybody else here was . . . white. It just felt really weird for me, like not being around other brown people. That's why I didn't come [often]." Shortly after, César, who is Latinx, started working at Spectrum, which made a big difference to Ernie and his experience. He started coming to the space more frequently and has since noticed that there are many more youth of color attending. Even though Spectrum, prior to César, was ostensibly a safe place for LGBTQ youth, its whiteness made it inaccessible to queer youth of color like Ernie. Another example of the way race intersects with sexuality and gender identities comes from Zia.

Zia, who describes herself as a "big, Black, bull dyke," is multiracial with coffee-colored skin and wears her hair in dreadlocks that stick out from under a knit cap. Today Zia is wearing a man's button-up shirt with a tie and vest, along with skinny jeans and sneakers. Her fingers are always wrapped in rings, her wrists in colorful bracelets. Zia has been coming to Spectrum for four years. Like Ernie, Zia describes the alienation of being queer within the lesbian community:

> Being weird and queer is probably, fucking, probably [*pause*] being weird was just hard as fuck. But being Black is just hard as fuck. And then you just add gay on top of that, and some other shit, it's just fucked. . . . And then it really comes to pressure, like, I can't be like ghetto and stuff [among white lesbians], and I like being ghetto 'cause I think it's funny, but it's like, you know when you're around . . . I guess sophisticated fondue? Like, "Look at me, I shop at Café Lesbian," it's like you have to be so, like, I guess proper. . . . You can't say like "fuck" or "shit" or, you know, none of that . . .

In addition to feeling like she can't be "ghetto" around particular white lesbians, she goes on to explain how among particular white, "hipster" activists, she gets accused of not being Black enough because her knowledge of hip-hop is lacking, while similarly, her queer lesbian identity results in her not being Black enough for "my own culture." While Travon shows how the term "queer" can be used to imply inclusiveness, an expansion of ways of being in the world, Ernie's and Zia's accounts suggest how they use "queer" to distinguish their experience from that of an LGBTQ mainstream.

Ferguson explains how patriarchal heteronormativity acts as a form of social control to define boundaries of, not just "normal" sexuality, but all normal ways of being in the world. His queer-of-color analysis "interrogates social formations as the intersections of race, gender, sexuality, and class, with particular interest in how those formations correspond with and diverge from nationalist ideas and practices."[11] Therefore, in U.S. society, one's race and class is integral to experiences of inclusion or exclusion. For white, cisgender, middle-class, able-bodied people, queerness—a marker of not belonging—is often limited to non-heterosexual displays of gender and sexuality or out-of-the-ordinary forms of heterosexuality like polyamory, the practice of being involved intimately with multiple people consensually, for example. All of the ways one cannot belong multiply for those who exist outside the middle and upper classes and who are not white, particularly dark-skinned people of color and some immigrants.

Yet simply being queer, as in "odd," "weird," or an outsider, is enough to trigger exclusion based on the raced, classed, and gendered aspects of heteronormativity. Jack is an example of a white, middle-class youth who has been marked throughout his life by queerness. An eighteen-year-old transman who identifies as pansexual but "leaning much more toward gay male," he spoke to me about the social risks of being different, something he referred to as "social death." Long before he started to publicly identify with LGBTQ identities, Jack understood himself to be different or queer. He says, "Well, I was already that weird nerd that no one would play *Magic* with. When the D&D nerds think you're too nerdy to play games with, you know . . ."[12] In addition to being "too nerdy," throughout his childhood Jack was gendered male by others so frequently that his mother was constantly on the defensive asserting that he was a girl. Although Jack grew up with the benefit of both white and middle-class privilege, he was intimately familiar with what it felt like to be queer.

The various ways young people deploy categories representing their sexualities and genders should also be read as a way for them to express

all of the complicated ways their other identities, along with lived experience, influence the labels they use to describe themselves. A young
person's choice of identity label says as much about their race, class, and
geographic location (to name a few categories) as it does about their
sexuality and/or gender.

As homosexuality becomes normalized in U.S. society, LGBTQ
people, community, and politics have gained mainstream recognition,
but some have argued that this access is limited to a particular kind of
LGBTQ subject.[13] For example, Lisa Duggan's concept, homonormativity, describes "an (LGBTQ) politics that does not contest dominant heteronormative assumptions and institutions, but upholds and sustains
them."[14] Homonormative politics allows some LGBTQ-identified people
to access heteronormative privilege, particularly those most willing to
disavow themselves of identity politics and civil rights agendas centered
around race, class, and gender. Further, concepts of heteronormativity
also raise questions about the existence of queer *heterosexualities*. Queer
heterosexualities are sexual behaviors that aren't monogamous, reproductive, and generally socially acceptable. These might include things
like engaging in bondage, discipline, and sadomasochism (BDSM);
being in non-monogamous or polyamorous relationships; and occupying other marginalized hetero identities. Therefore, my argument takes
into consideration that among LGBTQ-identified people, there are those
who have access to heteronormative privilege and those who, by way of
their queerness, do not. Similarly, straightness is heteronormative, but
heterosexuality can be queer.

Queer as an identity reflects active resistance to social expectations,
categorizations, and institutional control that continue to pit the normal
against the perverse. Queer exists alongside other identities like gay and
lesbian, not in place of them.[15] Yet the deployment of "queer" as a way
to describe what is not straight is not simply a matter of self-identity.
One can understand oneself as queer, as not fitting the contours of heteronormative society, but others also impose queer onto a subject, leaving them no choice in the matter. Sexuality is just one way people are
queered by society. One's race, gender, class, body size, nationality, and
ability can also be queered inasmuch as they exist outside the dominant
norm. Those queered members of society are typically not allowed access to the heteronormative mainstream, even if they want it. In other

words, there is a difference between self-identifying as queer and being queered by others, although the two can and do occur simultaneously. In the next section I look more closely at how sexual identity is formed in the context of LGBTQ community.

Discovering Queer Community

Gabe squeezed into the consultation room with me and the cardboard collection being stashed away for queer prom decorations. Gabe almost always wears a hat and has long brown hair. He sat in a chair with one ankle crossed over his knee, bouncing his foot throughout the interview. Gabe is an eighteen-year-old Latinx who identifies as bisexual and identifies his gender as androgynous. Gabe's friends use male pronouns to refer to him, and during check-in Gabe typically stated that he had no pronoun preference, so I use male pronouns for him here. Although he dresses mostly in masculine clothing and has a thin beard, his feminine-sounding voice and small stature lends him an appearance that often gets him mistaken for a girl. He describes being attracted to both boys and girls from early puberty, but prior to this moment had only dated girls. It was not until he had been introduced to the idea of bisexuality through his peer group at school that he came out as bisexual:

> It kind of start[ed] . . . during the end of elementary school, the beginning of middle school. And so, it's just, like, in the back of my mind I always thought, . . . "No, this isn't how it's supposed go. I shouldn't be thinking about guys that way, I should think about girls this way only." And . . . during middle school I was kind of, like, fighting myself on it a lot, but when I started high school and I got a chance to meet a whole lot of new people who were a part of the LGBTQ community, considering [my high school] was filled with so many, it just gave me a chance to just . . . stop and think and . . . be true to myself like, slap myself, "This is reality for you."

Although, prior to encountering the term "bisexual" and other members of the LGBTQ community, Gabe was experiencing same-sex desire, it was not until he was exposed to the idea through peers that he was able to name his experience, claim it as his own, and then begin exploring intimacy with male-identified persons.

I asked Fiona during our interview if she had any family members or close friends who were identified as LGBTQ. She explained that she was aware of no family members until she was older (as I mentioned above, her father identifies as pansexual), but she did have LGBTQ friends:

> In high school and middle school . . . I did start hanging out with . . . the gay kids and all of them. And we actually. . . . I sat in high school—every morning we sat in the same spot—and it became known to the rest of the school as the "Gay Wall," . . . but that was back when I actually still considered myself straight. But I actually hung out with them. I started hanging out with them in seventh and eighth grade, but I didn't really know about other sexual orientations until about freshman year. . . . Around sophomore, junior year I started identifying myself as bisexual. . . . They were just so much more fun than everyone else. They laughed. We just had a lot of fun. It was a really entertaining group to be with.

Across the country, the visibility of LGBTQ-identified young people in middle and high schools has been increasing.[16] Many middle and high schools today have gay-straight alliances and Pride centers, and youth centers like Spectrum exist in many communities. For some of the participants, it was exposure to other queer-identified young people that opened up opportunities for them to explore their own identities, something that previous generations were not able to do until they became adults, traveled to the geographical places where adult queer communities existed, and joined those communities themselves. As tolerance and awareness of LGBTQ-identified individuals and issues increase, sexual minority culture is validated in ways it never has been before. I saw this happen with many of the Spectrum young people, a group of whom had all attended the same public charter school where being LGBTQ-identified was relatively safe and supported not only by peers but by the teachers and administrators as well. This school, which Gabe attended, was just a few blocks away from Spectrum's previous location, and according to several of the people I spoke to, a large number of young people attending Spectrum also went to this school.

Both Gabe and Fiona describe finding an LGBTQ community among their peers. It is through these friend groups—with whom they both strongly identify—that they start to form language that better represents their own sexualities and genders. They learn from their peers what it means to be LGBTQ identified.

Anthony is a seventeen-year-old gay male who identifies as Hispanic. He is light-skinned, sometimes mistaken for white, he says, and on this particular day, his straight hair looks like a buzz cut in need of a trim. Anthony wears glasses, a polo shirt, and shorts. He is soft-spoken, yet confident, and exudes a strong sense of character and self-esteem throughout our interview. He speaks matter-of-factly and unabashedly about being gay. He has been coming to Spectrum since he was fourteen years old when his older, straight brother brought him for the first time. Anthony refers to his first boyfriend as a mentor, someone who helped him navigate the "gay world":

> My last relationship that I thought I was in love with somebody, it was with a guy named Thomas. . . . This was back when I first—or not first came out—but like a year after I'd first come out. And he was kind of like, my mentor in the gay world, showing me the ropes, getting me used to it, being my right-hand man as for comfort. So we got in a relationship and we got close. And it wasn't a long relationship, but [he] practically [became] my mentor in the GLBT community . . .

Miguel, like Anthony, also sought an out, gay boy in high school to date. Although he does not refer to his first boyfriend as a mentor the way Anthony does, his explanation for why he pursued him suggests that he admired this boy for being out and proud about his sexuality and was wanting to emulate that himself:

MARY: Was . . . he out and gay at school too?

MIGUEL: Um, yeah.

MARY: Were you out at school?

MIGUEL: Actually no. Oh, this is good . . . this is a good question. I was not out, and he was. And he was like the perfect model of everything that I wanted to embrace. . . . Me dating without having to worry about anybody judging me. And if they were judging me, I didn't care. And I wanted that.

MARY: Yeah. So he was boldly out.

MIGUEL: Yeah . . .

MARY: But that was attractive to you 'cause you couldn't be that?

MIGUEL: Yeah. And I was like, I want that so bad. I am here hiding myself . . . you know, from myself. And oh, suffering. And he's living the life that I wish I had.

Later, after Miguel broke up with this boyfriend and met his current boyfriend, the roles were reversed. He was now the out and proud gay boy and his new boyfriend was the one who was shy and afraid to be "out" in public. Then it was Miguel's turn to be the mentor.

Anthony spoke to me about how much he loves being gay: that his sexual identity is the most important part of his identity, the only part of his identity he says really cares about (compared to things like race or gender). He associates being gay with a particular type of personality or culture:

> I guess being at Spectrum, and being around peers that have . . . that are . . . allies to the community and also part of the community, so gays, lesbians, bi's, and all of them. . . . They're fun-loving people. So I've sort of taken myself as part of that community. So I see myself as a fun-loving, happy person. So that being in my sexuality base is kind of like . . . it's grown on me. So I kind of like how it feels. So for me being gay is really fun to me.

Anthony's description of the queer community belies one of the dominant discourses about LGBTQ youth as depressed and suicidal, raising an important point about the counterhegemonic role LGBTQ centers and communities play in U.S. society.

Finding a queer-oriented place like Spectrum was described as a pivotal moment for almost all of the participants in this study. They could finally let go of trying to make themselves fit into a heteronormative culture and instead find a place of belonging that was not only fun but also something to be proud of (a place to be queer). As Ward describes in *Not Gay*, "I discovered the object of my desire was not a person or even a class of people (like women or men), but queer spaces, queer ideas, and queer possibilities."[17]

Ditto, a twenty-one-year-old, biracial Latinx queer woman who identifies as bisexual, told me about how Spectrum was a place where she didn't feel judged, unlike high school, for example. In school, she said, "There was six weird people that we knew at the school that we were just the weird kids. We had these weird thoughts and everyone looked at us weird even though we were in the middle of downtown." She described her high school GSA as "mostly drama kids that were all pretending. . . . They were, like, 'We're here but . . . I'm just bi-curious,' but they would never actually be bi-curious." Ironically, it was while "ditching" a GSA meeting at school, which she described as "the boringest thing," that she discovered Spectrum for the first time. Describing Spectrum, she said, "The whole space was really colorful and I loved that it was . . . unless you knew someone that knew it, you didn't know it was there and it was some kind of [a] cool exclusive thing and I got to go and see that there was all these people and I wasn't a freak."

At Spectrum, youths are exposed through peers and workshops to ideas about how sexuality and gender exist on a spectrum and to a multitude of ways to identify oneself, including queer and pansexual. They also learn about the history of the LGBTQ rights movement and about queer culture like drag and Pride. All of this exposure validates the way they see themselves in the world, opening up new possibilities for ways of being. Ernie says:

> "I think . . . Spectrum definitely, like specifically César . . . kind of help me shape my sexuality, and where I was more comfortable. Or they help me find a place I was more comfortable in where . . . I'd have conversations with . . . César, about . . . if I date trans men does that make me straight because they're women? And stuff like that. . . . It shaped me 'cause it was able to put me in a place where I am comfortable."

César is the current program manager at Spectrum, having taken over for Sid not long after I started volunteering, and is the adult staff member with the most face-to-face contact with youths in the space. A gay Latinx in his mid-twenties, César is without question the most beloved member of the Spectrum community. He has a hip, asymmetrical haircut that often sports a lock of bright blue or purple, wears skinny jeans and high-top Vans-brand shoes, and possesses a bold confidence and brilliant charisma. César also has the advantage of being relatively young, in his early twenties, which means he can relate to the youth in the space in a meaningful way. Many of the kids at Spectrum really look up to him. César is loud and theatrical in the space and can command attention at the drop of a hat. During one sex-ed session, César used his own experience with the gender spectrum to explain his desires and identity. César nonchalantly explained that, while he had spent most of his life understanding himself as gay and only attracted to men, he had recently had moments where he found himself attracted to butch individuals who were not necessarily cisgender men. Therefore he was coming to realize that he was more attracted to masculinity than to men and therefore perhaps he was not as "gay" as he perhaps thought he was. This acknowledgment of fluidity and rejection of biological destiny by such an important Spectrum role model is a revolutionary act. Queer communities, like Spectrum, push the envelope of norms regarding sexuality and gender, so those particular young people, who have the opportunity to learn from mentors like César, form very different ideas about what it means to be gendered and sexual.

As I have shown here, we become sexual through processes of socialization. But this is not to suggest that one "chooses" their sexual orientation. Spectrum—and other communities like it—validates queer orientations. While heteronormativity as a straightening device is powerful, paying attention to the way people find themselves outside of the lines weakens notions of an innate hetero-homo binary. Although the LGBTQ rights movement has gained a lot of ground with bioessential explanations for sexuality, members of the same movement have troubled the waters of binary sexuality and gender for everyone to reckon with. Sexuality—in terms of how it is expressed, labeled, and experienced—is malleable and shifting and resists universal definition.

Not Born That Way

When I teach survey courses on gender and/or sexualities to students who are new to the subjects, one of the most difficult concepts for them to grasp is the idea that engaging in homosexual conduct does not necessarily make a person gay. They tilt their heads, scrunch up their faces, look around at others in the room for confirmation that they aren't the only ones confused by this notion. I think that one of the reasons they struggle is due to the success of the LGBTQ rights movement, which has resulted in the normalization and routinization of homosexuality in U.S. society.[18] My largely urban- and suburban-dwelling, Southern Californian students are increasingly recognizing same-sex couples and homosexuality as acceptable, and they have learned the proper language to use to identify someone who engages in homosexual behavior, relationships, and intimacy. Of course, many of those students themselves identify as lesbian, gay, bisexual, or queer. Among a lot of progressive, liberal-minded people—regardless of sexual identity—it is understood that same-sex conduct equals gay. Often, it is also understood that anyone who engages in same-sex conduct while still claiming to be straight is simply in denial of their gayness.[19]

Further, there is an underlying assumption at play here that often goes undetected in classroom conversation: that when we talk about what does and doesn't make a person gay, we seem to more often than not be talking about men. Society is more comfortable with the notion that women's sexuality is more fluid than men's, or at least that homosexual conduct among women does not, in all cases, make them gay.[20] Men are more vulnerable to the stigma of homosexuality if they engage in conduct that contradicts dominant gender norms. Therefore, not only will homosexual conduct result in others labeling a man as "gay," but there is a long litany of behaviors and affects that violate masculine norms that will also result in a "gay" label.[21]

Things are complicated further by the decades-long creep of a discourse that—also often in the name of LGBTQ rights—has successfully convinced many people that humans are born with an innate sexual orientation toward particular gendered others. According to the sociologist Tom Waidzunas, "To achieve a status of normality, the gay rights movement has increasingly conceptualized people in fixed sexual orientation boxes, shoring up a heterosexual/homosexual binary, and the movement has succeeded on this basis in many policy arenas."[22] Within this discourse, heterosexual desire is still considered the normative way to behave, while homosexual desire is likened to discovering that one has a birth defect or genetic anomaly, albeit one that is not your fault. The "born this way" discourse continues to reinforce the difference between heterosexuality and homosexuality, where heterosexuality is privileged. Even as the LGBTQ rights movement has, in many ways, successfully normalized homosexual conduct, gender, as the primary indicator of one's sexual attraction and identity, still holds sway. Many people continue to be preoccupied with sexual identity and how it aligns with gendered object choice, particularly when it comes to non-heterosexual sexual attractions.

It is an over-simplification to suggest that what makes a person gay is their same-sex sexual desire and/or behavior. While the youth of Spectrum often understand desire to be a key component to the formation of their sexual identities, there are several other factors at play, including failure to reproduce appropriate heterosexual scripts and gender nonconforming expression and behavior. This is important because not everyone who experiences same-sex sexual desire shares this childhood experience of difference. Similarly, not all people who identify as sexual minorities as adults experienced a homosexual sexual subjectivity as young people. Much of the "difference" described by Spectrum youth had to do with genderqueer expression and behavior, which helps to explain why those LGB-identified people who are gender-conforming often go "undetected" or aren't questioned about their sexuality.

Further, we learn from the youth of Spectrum that there are some who are rejecting identities that are defined by the gender of the bodies one desires. Identities like pansexual and queer allow youth to have a more open, fluid sexuality that is not confined strictly to whether one is engaging in heterosexuality or homosexuality. Queer is also a way to distance oneself from mainstream LGBTQ identities, identities that can be exclusive and homonormative.

Finally, young people described discovering LGBTQ community through peers and LGBTQ centers and beginning to form sexual and gender identities at this time. The youth of Spectrum describe finding refuge in LGBTQ communities where they have mentors to look up to, where they learn about the ways that difference can be valued rather than disparaged, and most important, where they learn that they are not alone in their queerness. By validating difference, Spectrum offers refuge for young people who struggle to find a sense of belonging at school and in their communities. These young people are rejected by, and reject, the dominant norm; they are queer-oriented youth. The next chapter explores how the queer youth of Spectrum negotiate transgender phenomena. Whereas LGBTQ youth centers were once largely populated by kids experiencing same-sex desire and the resulting social sanctions that accompany that, genderqueerness may now be the more defining characteristic of these spaces.

3

"Let's Be Trans"

Going beyond the Gender Binary

"Let's do check-in, y'all!" César, Spectrum's program director, hollers over the din of the music pouring out of the speakers. We approach the overstuffed armchairs that form a circle on a rug in the center of the space. Under strings of multicolored holiday lights made nearly invisible by competing day-bright fluorescents, a motley crew of adult staff, volunteers, interns, and youths slowly come together, quieting down for the daily ritual known as "check-in." On some days, the number of adults in the space awkwardly outnumbers that of youth; on others, the youth dominate, and the group spills over to the benches that surround the chairs, more filtering in as check-in proceeds. César, with a flick of his black, asymmetrical bangs, commands attention with ease, and the various side-conversations die down quickly as he begins to speak:

> Welcome to Spectrum, a safe space for lesbian, gay, bisexual, transgen-
> der, queer and questioning youth and their allies. We don't care how you
> identify, just that you are down with queer liberation [*to which those of
> us in the know raise our "claws" and say, "RAWR!"*]. We're going to do a
> little thing called check-in where you tell us your name—doesn't have to
> be your real name—your preferred gender pronoun—examples of pro-
> nouns are things like "he" and "she," but you can also use gender neutral
> pronouns like "ze," "they," or "hir"—let us know how your day is going.
> Who has a question of the day?

It is within this daily practice of checking-in that youth and adults alike are socialized into the queer milieu that is Spectrum, the process serving both as an initiation for first-timers and a time-honored ritual for regulars. Undoubtedly, the question most likely to stump people new to the space is the one referring to the preferred gender pronoun

(PGP).[1] In most social spaces, people do not take the time to explain to others the gender pronouns they use to identify themselves; it is taken for granted to be obvious. Yet gender is not obvious for everyone. In addition to being a safe place for youth to explore non-heteronormative sexualities, Spectrum is a safe place for genderqueerness. Processes like sharing one's PGP among the group effectively disrupts the invisible work that naturalizes gender. People may ask to be referred to by female pronouns like "she" and "her" or male pronouns like "he" and "him." Alternately, gender neutral pronouns like "they," which can be used to refer to an individual person without signifying a binary gender, and other gender neutral pronouns like "ze" or "hir" are offered up as options for how to refer to a person without using a name. At Spectrum, not only can you be someone who embodies genderqueerness and still be recognized, but you can also be a gender normative person who plays around with using different pronouns. By queering gender in this way, the effect is to reorient the possibilities of what a gendered person can do and be. In *Queer Phenomenology*, Sara Ahmed says, "Gender is an effect of the kinds of work that bodies do, which in turn 'directs' those bodies, affecting what they 'can do."[2] What happens when you challenge society's ideas about what a gendered body can do?

Queer-oriented spaces like Spectrum are utopian in their willingness and ability to reimagine gender, if not undo it entirely. In her book, *Undoing Gender*, the gender theorist Judith Butler talks about how "fantasy is what allows us to imagine ourselves and others otherwise."[3] The possibility for social transformation can be located in the moments in which norms are disrupted. Butler refers back to her work on drag—as well as nods to the contemporary transgender movement—to argue that these ways of bending gender are political, "by not only making us question what is real, and what has to be, but by showing us how contemporary notions of reality can be questioned, and new modes of reality instituted."[4] Similarly, in *Cruising Utopia*, queer theorist José Esteban Muñoz speaks of queerness as an ideality. For Muñoz, the hope lies in the striving toward queerness, not necessarily the accomplishment of it: "What we need to know is that queerness is not yet here but it approaches like a crashing wave of potentiality."[5] At Spectrum, where there is an institutionalized effort to recognize cisgender privilege and support the trans* movement, gender—along with sexuality—has become particularly salient component of youth identity. Spectrum's approach to gender shows us the potentiality of queerness.

Transgender Phenomena

In Spectrum, I think it's very accepting. I never even heard, until I came here, or even thought about asking somebody about their gender, their pronoun preference. Never, never ever in any place, and I get that every time, every time people come, like, even when I ask something they're like what are you talking about? When I meet somebody new, I'm like, "What's your pronoun preference?" And I'm like, "Yeah, well, what do you identify?" And people out in the street . . . I've had trans people who like, don't pass, be like, "Thank you for asking." But it's something . . . I love about that. We're very trans inclusive.
—Ernie, twenty-one-year-old, queer Chicanx

While gender has long been a matter of concern in LGBTQ communities, rethinking the use of gender pronouns and the adoption of a gender identity—in addition to a sexual identity—are indicators of a new way of thinking about sexuality and gender. Young people coming of age during the rise of trans* awareness have witnessed increasing exposure to trans* experience, including high-profile trans*-identified celebrities and countless news stories about trans*-identified children and youth, and among their peers, they are experiencing a proliferation of gender identities beyond the binary male/female. The young people coming of age today are living with a different phenomenological experience of gender than those who came of age before them; they are experiencing transgender phenomena. According to the transgender studies scholar Susan Stryker, "transgender phenomena, in short, point the way to a different understanding of how bodies mean, how representation works, and what counts as legitimate knowledge."[6]

It was simply not the case that the teenagers in the 1980s, when I grew up in a flyover city in the western United States, formed gender identities that required discussing gender pronouns, regardless of one's ontological understanding of their gender. We did have names for sexual orientations and identities, and we had the term "straight" as a way to begin to understand that heterosexuality was as much a sexual orientation as homosexuality. This was radically different compared to our parents, who would have only understood two options for one's sexuality *and* gender, normal or queer (meaning queer in a derogatory sense). But the generation that the youth of Spectrum belong to, those born after 1990 or so, have largely grown up in a culture in which homosexuality is relatively normalized and gender identity is becoming as prevalent a part of the formation of self as sexuality. While I do not think that most of the people in this generation have widely accepted transgender, gender fluidity, and gender non-conformity—familiarity and acceptance varies widely, particularly by geographical area and region—they are, as a group, exposed to transgender phenomena in a way that previous generations were not.

Although the mainstream emphasis on trans* experience reifies transitions from one gendered body to another, transgender phenomena are not simply about transbinary experiences. By focusing particularly on the experiences of how young people experience gender ambiguity, in this chapter I show how the youth of Spectrum complicate gender beyond the binary. For these young people, gender identity is a process of self-recognition and peer influence that is complicated by how others attribute their gender and is often mired in ambivalence. Below, I share some more detailed experiences of genderqueer youths in order to demonstrate how being ambiguously gendered/sexed is a complicated— while not altogether troublesome—experience.

Contextualizing Gender

While spaces like Spectrum are often associated with sexuality and sexual identities, trans* people have always occupied LGB spaces. Trans* activists have been hard at work pushing for the recognition of trans* rights within the sexual rights movement. They have had to remind the larger cisgender LGB community to accept that people with trans* experience have always been part of the movement yet to also understand how the needs of trans* people are in many ways distinct from the needs of sexual minority groups.[7] It's important to understand that sexual identity is not always the most salient identity among the kids who frequented Spectrum.

By way of example, Spectrum participates in a statewide queer youth conference every year. During the conference I attended a workshop on trans* identity that featured members of Spectrum's community. During the question-and-answer period, Jaime, one of Spectrum's peer staff who is cismale, spoke up, explaining that he always thinks about coming out as being about sexuality, not gender, and he wanted to know what Jack, a Spectrum regular who is transmale, thought was different about coming out as trans* as opposed to coming out as gay. Jack responded that there was a point in his experience where he really made it much more about gender than sexuality because his biggest fear was that people would react to the fact that he was a trans* male who liked men by asking him why he didn't just stay a straight female? People who are naïve about trans* experiences often get caught up in this very conflation, and resulting confusion, of sexuality and gender.

Often the youth of Spectrum conflated sex, sexuality, and gender, therefore my observations of and interviews with youths about their sexualities were almost always also about their gender. Many times during interviews, when I asked people to tell me their sexual identity, they might say "male," or when I asked what their gender identity was, they'd say, "gay." The ethnographer in me was never sure whether to correct them, although I usually ended up giving them some sort of hint as to the difference between gender and sexuality, as I had intended it. But the confusion that occurs when trying to distinguish between the two is evidence of the interrelatedness of sexuality and gender.

It is difficult to separate gender from sexuality because of the way one signifies the other in a semiotic sense. The fact of Jack's experience, where others automatically assume his gender identity is directly related to his sexual identity, is a good example of this. The sociologist James Dean, in his book *Straights*, explains the increasing importance of gender identity: "Gender identity practices, then, have taken on a renewed importance in sexual identity practices and politics. Since gender identity practices are the grid for a heterosexual/homosexual sign system that is overlaid on them, masculine/feminine practices have become a key site and structure for the performance of sexual identity and straight and gay identity politics."[8] The reality is that each of us likely experiences our gender and sexuality as deeply intertwined, and similarly we tend to ascribe sexual identities based on gender expression or behavior and vice versa.[9]

This study began during a moment in history in which the first generation of trans*-identified children is being reared.[10] Where pointed discussions about gender identity were once only the purview of LGBTQ-friendly and trans*-friendly spaces, gender talk is increasingly becoming mainstream. Thanks to several high-profile cases, the visibility and awareness of trans* people are on the rise. While I was doing my fieldwork at Spectrum from 2010 to 2013, feature stories about trans* children ran in both the *Washington Post* and the *New York Times*,[11] and high-profile figures like Lara Jane Grace of the rock band Against Me! and Lana Wachowski, co-director of *The Matrix* film franchise, came out publicly as trans*. In the subsequent years since I conducted my research, trans* issues have seen an unprecedented volume of media attention, the most high profile cases of which have been transwomen Laverne Cox and Caitlyn Jenner. It is not uncommon to see posters on college campuses that state, "What gender do you prefer?" along with a list of options. Another strong indicator of a sea change taking place is that, in 2015, the *Washington Post* officially changed its style guide to allow for writers to refer to individuals using the gender neutral pronoun "they."[12]

In addition to trans* awareness, increasingly more people—especially young people—are adopting "genderqueer" and "gender fluid" (along with fluid sexualities) as terms to describe gender that does not conform to the female/male, feminine/masculine binary. Social media plays an important part in the shifting norms around gender as people across the globe are having real-time discussions and debates about gender, trans* issues, and queer sexualities on forums like Tumblr, Twitter, and Facebook. A favorite celebrity role model of LGBTQ youth, Miley Cyrus, stated in a *Paper Magazine* interview during summer of 2015, "I don't relate to being boy or girl, and I don't have to have my partner relate to boy or girl."[13] Yet society is so deeply socialized into a binary gender order that the process of gender attribution, the act of determining whether someone is a boy or a girl the first time we see them, is difficult to disrupt.[14]

While young people, like Cyrus, may embrace the idea of gender fluidity, culturally the dominant social norms around gender continue to
reproduce the binary. It's one thing to embrace a gender-fluid identity,
but actually embodying an ambiguous gender may result in a hostile
climate—both in and outside of the LGBTQ community. For those kids
whose gender does not conform to society's norms, the process of forming a gender identity is complicated, not only by how they understand
themselves but also by how others perceive them. Because of the intertwining relationship of gender and sexuality, discomfort around gender
ambiguity is often tied to how it troubles taken-for-granted assumptions
about how gender determines sexuality (as discussed in the previous
chapter).

Grappling with Each Other's Gender

Adam is an eighteen-year-old, white, gay, cisgender man with rosy,
freckled skin and strawberry blond hair who embodies feminine characteristics like a soft, round face and body. While we talk, he gesticulates
his hands and arms animatedly and can transform into a bawdy show-
girl at the drop of a hat. When I ask him what he thinks other people
usually assumed his gender to be, he responds, "That's a really good
question. A lot of people . . . first mistake me for a girl for a second. And
then they realize that I'm a guy." Jude, a twenty-two-year-old, white
transwoman who identifies as pansexualtransplus, is tall, thin, and fair
skinned. Her hair is dark with blond-highlighted tips, and she parts it
off center, with one side of her bangs hanging in her face. She and I had
a quiet visit one afternoon in the interns' office. She was temporarily
living in town and had sought out Spectrum, knowing that LGBTQ
communities are typically safe spaces for trans people to be. Although
her voice and muscle tone suggest maleness, she evokes female-
supermodel androgyny. Similarly to Adam, she explains, "I think most
people perceive my gender—if they haven't already asked—um, then
they're gonna assume male most of the time. I've had some people identify it as androgynous. . . . They have difficulty placing it." Both Adam
and Jude are describing how others attribute their gender. In fact, you
can see my own process of gender attribution in the way I describe
their gender expression. Gender attribution is the process by which

a "perceiver" assigns gender to a "displayer," based on secondary and tertiary sex characteristics like body size, location and characteristics of body hair, voice, facial expression, movement, and body posture, as well as non-essential extra-body characteristics like clothing, makeup, and hairstyle.[15]

Spectrum engages in various practices to make the process of attribution more visible. For example, asking youth to identify their PGP and holding everyone accountable for then using the right pronoun when referring to each other is one way to disrupt the process of gender attribution. If people learn not to rely strictly on their attribution of others' gender and instead allow others to self-identify their gender, it makes the process of attribution more visible. This has the effect of encouraging a climate in which gender identity becomes an important aspect of self-expression and understanding for everyone in the space, regardless of their gender. Potentially, it might help us call into question many of the assumptions we make about gendered hierarchies. This is not to say that the PGP question removes inequalities among gendered people, but it opens up an opportunity to interrogate gender. But of course, inequality persists, between masculine and feminine people, as well as between cisgender and trans* gender people.

For those who take for granted their gender and therefore never question their preferred gender pronoun, being asked to identify it can be rather flummoxing. For Spectrum attendees, check-in is likely the first time they have heard someone talk so explicitly about gender. Newcomer reactions to this topic are generally mixed, ranging from simple confusion to awkward laughter. The first time I had to share my PGP I misspoke and said, "I prefer he/she pronouns," much to my embarrassment (I use and respond to female pronouns). I was not alone in my awkward nervousness when it came to answering this question, as this field note demonstrates:

> There was a young woman at Spectrum yesterday, one of the Goth kids, who, when she introduced herself, instead of saying what gender pronouns she preferred stated that she was bi. I've never heard anyone identify their sexual orientation at check-in, so I think it was a combination of her being nervous and confusing sexual identity with gender identity.

Beyond the awkwardness of grappling with one's PGP, being put into a position of having to think about it often starts important conversations about gender, trans* individuals, and cisgender privilege, as demonstrated by an incident I noted involving a newcomer to Spectrum, a cisgender boy with short, curly hair dyed purple and lipstick to match:

> During check-in when it got to him, in response to gender pronouns he stated that he didn't want to offend anyone, but that he calls everyone "girl" and was that okay? He said he'd been at Burger King earlier in the day and called someone "girl" who got really angry with him.

I have no way of knowing the gender identity of the person whom he referred to as "girl" at Burger King, nor do I know the rest of the story, but as check-in made its way around the circle, Mark—a transmale youth with boy-short brown hair, dressed in the typical male adolescent uniform of a T-shirt, jeans, and sneakers—made his feelings clear about this topic when he said, "I prefer male pronouns and I *will* get upset if you refer to me as a female." This is not an uncommon occurrence. Often, those in the space have to confront their assumptions and prejudices, like having to think about why gay men's practice of calling everyone "girl" might be problematic as some youths are explicitly striving to not be recognized as a girl.

Although the practice of sharing PGPs during check-in is meant to alert everyone in the space to be mindful of people's identities, there continue to be slipups. Those youth whose gender is difficult for others to place confound the gender attribution process. This can result in the frustrating and hurtful frequency of having their gender misappropriated, even after they have announced their PGP. For example, I noted this particular exchange between a cisgender female youth and Adrian, a graduate student intern who is a transman, prefers male gender pronouns, but embodies some secondary and tertiary feminine sex/gender characteristics like a feminine sounding voice:

> Later, Saffron referred to Adrian as "she" and César again called her out and said, "Adrian uses male pronouns." Saffron looked right at Adrian and said she remembered him saying that at check-in. "Do you hate me?" I didn't hear Adrian's answer.

While among regulars at Spectrum Adrian is generally properly gendered male, newcomers would often misgender him as female. Similarly, I found it to frequently be the case that people in the space would forget to use gender neutral pronouns such as "they" for those who stated that preference during check-in. Unless the individual really worked hard to remind others to use gender neutral pronouns, most people would fall back into using binary pronouns pretty quickly. As the practice of acknowledging pronouns becomes more widespread, the use of gender neutral pronouns is sure to become more common, but as I show here with Adrian—who wants to be referred to by male pronouns—using "they" to refer to him is not necessarily acceptable.[16]

This may or may not be the generation who breaks through the confines of binary gender to a place where gender ambiguity or a third or multiple ways of being gendered is embraced. They most certainly seem to be laying the groundwork by adopting gender neutral identities and pronouns and working at resisting binaries, but what I describe here is not reflective of a mainstream movement yet. The power of binary gender is hard to escape. As the sociologist Betsy Lucal explains in her reflection on what it is like living as a woman who embodies masculine characteristics, "We cannot escape doing gender or, more specifically, doing one of two genders."[17] But perhaps within spaces like Spectrum, where a concerted effort is being made to disrupt the gender binary, ambiguity can more safely occur.

Being Gendered by Others

Many have documented elsewhere that the medical pathologizing of transsexual and transgender persons has necessitated that individuals seeking medical or surgical transition comply with an origin story that somehow proves how they know they are the wrong gender.[18] According to the American Psychiatric Association, the *Diagnostic and Statistical Manual of Mental Disorders* (*DSM-5*) describes gender dysphoria as "a difference between one's experienced/expressed gender and assigned gender, and significant distress or problems functioning."[19] A formal gender dysphoria diagnosis from a doctor is often necessary for health insurance plans to cover medical and surgical procedures that would otherwise be determined elective. As more and more young people are identifying publicly as trans*, explanations rooted in biological or psychological—as opposed to sociological—origins reinforce this narrative of being assigned the wrong gender at birth or a child insisting that they are one gender stuck in the wrongly gendered/sexed body. Without negating the lived experience of those who *do* experience their gender this way, of the several trans* youth I came to know at Spectrum, very few of them describe their experience as being trapped in the wrong body. Most of them describe a process of recognition that paralleled the onset of puberty, sexual awakening, and the development of other identities.

Like all of the transmale youths I interviewed at Spectrum, Spencer came out as a lesbian (he told me this while enclosing the word "lesbian" in finger quotes) before he came out as trans*. As discussed in a previous chapter, gender non-conformance is often assumed to be a signifier of homosexuality, and it was not unusual for transmale-identified youth at Spectrum to have first come out to others as lesbians or gay before realizing that, for them, it was their gender, not their sexuality, that they were negotiating. Spencer once explained that he met a girl in middle school who asked him, "Do you really want to be a girl?" He replied that he did not and she said, "Let's be trans." Similarly, other youths' explanations of their acquisition of gender identity reflect how the influence of peers and others who share similar experiences were crucial to their identity formation. Jude, for example, shared how she learned about trans* through an online gaming community she belonged to where, over time, members of the group began to disclose their trans* identities to each other. In a different case, Adam shared with me, looking back on his late childhood, that he believes that had he known being trans* was an option, he likely would have grown up to be a girl.

The narrative of being trapped in the wrong body takes for granted that there is such a thing as an authentic trans* person (or authentic gendered person, for that matter) and it is rooted in the assumption that one is either born a boy or a girl but that, in a small number of cases, biology somehow got it wrong. Conversely, anyone who cannot prove the origin of their sense of wrongness, or whose gender identity is not fixed but fluid, is not seen as legitimate. Therefore the assumption that there is a right or a wrong way to "be" gendered dismisses the experiences of ambiguity that complicate gendered experiences. The pathological model forecloses on any opportunity to understand gender ambiguity as normal and healthy. But not all genderqueer people are interested in transitioning gender or even in identifying as trans*, for that matter; many of them will live their lives occupying the ambiguous space in between.

Among the genderqueer and trans* youth participants, many spoke of their struggles with gender at school, at home, on the street, and among peers. Spencer, first mentioned above, is a nineteen-year-old Latinx with the voice of a boy and who typically identifies as male at check-in. He is quite short and wears dark, bulky clothes like long-sleeved T-shirts hanging down to his knees, too-big jeans dragging at the heels, and a wallet chain swinging at his hip. He keeps his dark, curly hair short, sometimes shaving his head. He has braces, and although he's supposed to wear glasses he doesn't because he claims the combination of glasses and braces "fuck with my game." Walking to the park together one day, Spencer christened the illuminated walking man at the crosswalk "Transman," then he said, "FTM Man," to be specific, which is how I learned Spencer had been assigned a female gender at birth. Spencer explained that he has an information-processing disorder and has attended several high schools. He said, "Schools don't get me," referring to his gender status. He also told me about how his mother, who has made some effort to use his male name and refer to him using male pronouns at home, referred to him by his "girl" name at a family funeral. She describes him as being a "tomboy," rather than referring to him as a man. He stated angrily that he hasn't been a tomboy since he was eleven and that it was insulting to him to have people see him as a girl. He kept insisting that he wanted to be recognized as a guy and not a tomboy and that he wanted to be taken seriously.

Jack, an eighteen-year-old white transmale who identifies as "pansexual but leaning towards gay," says he now passes for male in most situations. He wears small, wire-frame glasses and, in the winter, an orange Carhartt-brand jacket. Jack, who did most of the talking while I listened attentively, is quite comfortable sharing his experiences with others, especially in the interest of raising awareness. He is an evangelical Christian and feels that he has an obligation to do as Jesus challenges him, to share his experiences as a transman with others. He refers to a parable from the Bible, "Why, if you were given a lamp, why would you hide it under a bush?"[20] He sees his reality as a queer person as the lamp he should not hide and that he should be out, shining the way for others. When I ask him how others read his gender, he claims that he appears to most people "like your typical working-class dude." He recounts how in high school he struggled to get teachers and other administrative staff to refer to him using male pronouns owing to the fact that all of his official documentation identifies him as a girl. Even though in most cases he was being read male, he explains, "The professors would always correct people. I don't know if they thought they were being helpful or . . . most people who, like, correct people are just being helpful, but I felt like it wasn't being helpful. It was almost a power thing."

Taylor is a white, eighteen-year-old transwoman who identifies as a pansexual female and dresses like a glam rocker from the 1970s in heeled, knee-high boots, dark clothes, torn shirts covered in netting, and black eyeliner around her piercing blue eyes. Taylor grew up in an abusive family and was hospitalized many times as a youth, initially for drug abuse and cutting, later in attempts to "cure" her of gender dysphoria. She had recently fled her hometown, where her mother made her life as a transwoman untenable. She followed a Facebook friend to this town and is currently staying in a shelter for homeless youth. The day we spoke, her blond hair was dyed black and worn short and spiky. When asked what most people think her gender is, Taylor explains that she is most often taken for male:

> Most people . . . when I'm walking down the street, I'll have two or three people, every time I do it, walk up and say, "I like your look, brother." So people just seem to think I'm just a hardcore rocker guy. Cause I wear black, I've got the high heels with the belts, I'm just, I don't know. I don't mind it, but I really wish I could, you know, make people see me as a woman more.

These accounts show how at school, on the street, or among family, youth are negotiating gender. At school these gender non-conforming youth are, as Judith Butler describes in *Gender Trouble*, unintelligible.[21] In situations with authority figures, youths have to consider how they are being perceived—what gender others are attributing them—in order to negotiate interactions. Among family, youths have to struggle against fixed gender attributions, often with little or no help from family members to reimagine their gender. In her reflection on her own gender ambiguity, Lucal describes, "How I see myself, even how I might wish others would see me, is socially irrelevant. It is the gender that I appear to be (my perceived gender) that is most relevant to my social identity and interactions with others."[22] Gender attribution intrudes upon the private experience of one's gender identity because no matter how one personally identifies, without affirmation from others, the opportunity to be recognized as that gender—binary or otherwise—becomes less attainable.

Experiencing Ambivalence

While the youths at Spectrum who identified as trans* were in various stages of transition, many lived their day-to-day lives as the gender they identified with and were successfully passing as that gender in most cases.[23] They were deeply invested in their trans identities and talked a lot about the significance this experience had had and continued to have on their lives. Spencer talked about being a "regular guy," or about "guys like me," or "I'm not that kind of guy," when he is referring to girls and dating. Jack told me it is important to him to identify as a transmale, but stated, "Most people don't think I'm trans*, I think at this point everybody thinks I'm male." About his gender identity, Rick, a nineteen-year-old white male, stated, "I've been passing about one hundred percent of the time since this time last year. Like after I went to college and there were no people who knew me before I was male, I passed as male one hundred percent of the time. Usually as a gay man, but passing as male."

It surprised me one day when Spencer—who had been so adamant about his male identity in all of our previous exchanges, showed up one day wearing eye makeup, fingernail polish, and a feminine blouse and shoes, hand-in-hand with a girl. He explained to me that with some people his boy comes out and with some people his girl comes out and that "his girl had been coming out for the first time in forever" because he'd been spending time with a lesbian friend. Spencer shared with me many times that he had very strong feelings for this girl, but their relationship had most recently been on the rocks. Now that they were hanging out again, was Spencer feeling some pressure to align his gender with her sexual identity as lesbian? Not only are youths influenced by their relationships with others, but, as Spencer's experience demonstrates, the logic of the sexual order—an order that now includes same-sex sexualities like lesbian and gay—simply does not always fit their own understanding of themselves as gendered, sexual beings.

Embodying Gender Ambiguity

One can easily perform gender in a myriad of ways by simple alterations of dress, makeup, facial and body hair, and body movements, but there are certain embodied characteristics that cannot easily be transformed without hormonal or surgical treatments, if at all. These include the sound of a person's voice, body size and shape (including, for example, having breasts or the size and shape of one's hands), and location and thickness of facial and body hair. Some people's gender expression is very masculine or feminine, but most of us fall somewhere along a spectrum of gender characteristics: some closer, others further away from those polarities. Jude expressed that although she is doing hormone replacement therapy, she would rather embody an androgynous than a female gender.[24] She sums up nicely how she recognizes her own gender on a spectrum: "In fact, I would say pretty commonly the direct ratio of male to female, uh, stereotypically based on social constructs of the gender binary, would be about twenty-three [male]: seventy-seven [female]."

But there are those people whose gender expression is quite androgynous, and they experience others always questioning whether they are a boy or a girl. Not only are these individuals subject to policing of their sexuality, as social norms result in a conflation of sexuality and gender, but they are further sanctioned for not fitting into appropriate gender norms.

There are a handful of youths at Spectrum that I refer to as ambiguously gendered for whom the PGP question is helpful because it allows them the opportunity to identify as they want to be identified, not as others decide for them. As I mentioned previously, it also eases the discomfort of those around them who are unsure of their gender, and unlike the cisgender youth, they are more likely to get mis-identified both inside and outside the space. For clarity, I understand these particular youths to be people who (1) are more or less comfortable identifying with the gender that aligns with the sex they were assigned at birth even though they embody a gender that often contradicts that identity, or (2) prefer to identify as genderqueer or gender fluid because their embodiment and expression of gender is ambiguous. Although one could describe youths in either category as trans* in that their gender expression fits under the umbrella the term is meant to encompass, the youths described below did not identify as trans*.

Corey, an eighteen-year-old Latinx who identifies their gender using the term "universal" and their sexuality using the term "energy," has a very unique style. For our interview they had on a T-shirt with the sleeves cut off, along with two leather studded belts, one worn around their waist and the other worn like backpack straps over their shoulders. Corey wore pink running shorts over dark leggings, one side of which were torn open. On their feet were fuzzy, thick neon ankle socks and no shoes. They wore Wayfarer-style sunglasses throughout our interview, so I could only barely make out their eyes. When I asked Corey to clarify their gender identity, they said, "You know, I just, with gender references, I really just don't think of male or female for myself. It's just me." Corey explains how they are understood as femme within the LGBTQ community and how they often confuse people in the broader community when it comes to their gender:

> Well, I know in the LGBTQ community . . . they think I'm really feminine and really flamboyant, and very, uh, "twinkie," you know? So, it's . . . depending on where I'm at. 'Cause even . . . like going on the bus, people will probably think that—from the way that I dress and um . . . how I bring myself out, I guess you'd say—I don't know what they would think. I think that's exactly what they think . . . is they don't know, you know? It's like, well, I don't know.

I was often struck by the irony that some youths at Spectrum so easily passed—and therefore were mistaken—for another gender than the one with which they identify, while others who wanted to transition from one gender to another found it hard to pass as they desired. The difference has to do with how one embodies gender and therefore how others attribute gender to them. I use "embodiment" in an attempt to distinguish more fixed gender characteristics—for example, secondary and tertiary sex/gender characteristics like the sound of one's voice or the location and amount of body hair—from "gender expression," which is the multifaceted ways that each and every one of us can choose to display our gender to others, including clothing, makeup, hairstyles, mannerisms, and more. But, of course, embodiment could be understood as a form of gender expression.

Gabe is an eighteen-year-old bisexual Latinx who is about five-and-a-half feet tall and slight of frame. He typically dresses in masculine clothing like blue jeans, hiking shoes, and T-shirts. He wears his dark brown, wavy hair long, usually highlighted some shade of red. He has a soft, feminine face but almost always has a beard of dark hair that grows just up to his throat and over his chin and jaw bone, but not up the side of his face. More notable even than his feminine facial features and small stature is his voice, which sounds very much like that of a young woman. He is overall gentle, soft-spoken, and kind. Gabe claims no gender pronoun preference during check-ins and introduces himself both as Gabe and as his alter ego, Kaylee. I have never heard anyone refer to him as anything other than Gabe and using male pronouns, indicating that among his friends he is attributed a male gender. Outside of Spectrum, though, he is often mistaken for a woman. After telling me this in an interview, I asked him how he feels about being identified as a woman by strangers, and he explained:

> It actually makes me feel happy, knowing that, even when I'm not trying, like, people will think that I'm a woman. And it's just, like sometimes, it kind of grinds my gears, 'cause sometimes I'll be dressed completely like a boy. I'm wearing a nice button-up shirt, some good jeans, it's just like, I'm obviously wearing—I mean, I own more boy shoes than I do girl shoes—it's just like, I go out completely dressed and looking like a guy and I even have facial hair and everything and yet I still have somebody mistake me for a woman. And sometimes I'm just like, "Grrr, like hello? Do you not see the facial hair? Does it look like I have breasts?" [laughs]. So like, it's kind of bittersweet sometimes but most of the time I just feel happy knowing that I can get people to think that I'm a woman without even trying.

Using secondary (non-reproductive, physical characteristics) and tertiary (non-verbal behaviors such as facial expression, movement, body posture) sex/gender characteristics, people find it difficult to categorize Gabe's gender because of the ways that his ambiguity defies a clearly male or female gender. As described above, Gabe does not seem bothered by his gender ambiguity. In addition to his experiences with strangers who think he is a woman, he also likes to perform in Spectrum's drag shows, and his embodiment of gender makes it easier for him to pass as a woman, which results in various symbolic and material rewards in a space where being a man who can successfully pass as a woman in a performance setting is highly valued.

Another example of a genderqueer youth is Ditto, a twenty-year-old bisexual, biracial Latinx who is six feet tall and, in her own words, "fat." The first time I ever saw Ditto, she was performing at the drag show. She performed "Cannibal Queen" by the indie pop band Miniature Tigers. She wore a tiny top hat on her head and swung a cane around as she walked up and down the runway. Her face was made up to look like her lips were stitched shut and fake blood dripped out of her mouth while she lip synced the words: "Comin' for your heart like a cannibal / Oh, she lets me right in and I'm fed 'til I'm full / If something goes wrong, I'm accountable / Oh, a life without her is no life at all." At check-in, Ditto is likely to say that she does not care what gender pronouns are used to refer to her. In our interview she explained that she has a disorder that causes her to have ambiguous gender traits, and that, along with her size, makes people question her gender. When I asked about her gender identity she offered this account:

DITTO: I am predominantly female, sometimes I'm genderqueer.
MARY: And people out in the world, people who don't know you personally, how do you think they perceive your gender?
DITTO: Uh, a lot of people just don't know. I have a chemical imbalance, so sometimes I'll grow facial hair and so people question then, too. They're like, "I don't know if that's a fat guy or a hairy girl." So, I just throw people off with my gender all the time.
MARY: So people are confused by it a lot.
DITTO: Yes, a lot of times I just hear "freak" and that's fine.

People like Corey, Gabe, and Ditto, who embody an ambiguous gender, did not describe feelings of gender dysphoria to me. Their self-identification is not in contradiction with the gender they were assigned at birth.[25] Even in the case of Jude, who is undergoing hormone therapy and identifies as a woman, she says, "I just want to be like a female that dresses like a guy." For these young people, ambiguity is the norm, not a moment of transition. Being genderqueer, however, is not just about those people who want to change their gender identity and expression: It includes people who live entire lives of gender ambiguity. Trans* people encompass a diverse variety of individuals and experiences, from those who have successfully transitioned from one gender to another within the binary, to those who are in the midst of that process or want to be, but also to those who are in the spaces in between. As with any community of people striving for legitimacy in larger society, there are rifts and divisions among the trans* community that are often based on authenticity or successful achievement of transition. But largely, the trans* movement has embraced the idea of opening gender up for interpretation beyond the binary.[26] And it is important to state that not everyone who embodies gender ambiguity or who plays in non-binary realms of gender expression identify as trans*.

Consequences of Ambivalent Gender

Genderqueer youth are exceptionally marginalized because their very presence disrupts the seemingly natural gendered order of things. Those youths who do not fit into the gender binary struggle with being understood at school, at home, and on the street. They are labeled "disruptive," "learning disabled," "mentally ill," "delinquent," or, in hate language, "freak." Yet the youth of Spectrum are living in an age where gender is being challenged in a new way. They are more likely to understand gender as fluid rather than immutable. They potentially have access to new technologies in the form of clothing, makeup, wigs, hair removal, hormones, and surgeries that make it easier than ever to physically transform the embodied aspects of one's gender. Being genderqueer is nothing new, but the expanded possibilities and options for transition and expression have grown immensely. Along with this, the possibilities for gender identity have expanded as well.

Spectrum has played a crucial role in the lives of genderqueer youths who face certain bullying and harassment, as well as other forms of social sanction, for not conforming to society's expectations of looking and acting like typical boys and girls. By institutionalizing the disruption of gender—asking people to identity their PGP, for example—Spectrum allows for non-binary, ambiguous genders to be recognized. It has allowed Gabe, Ditto, and Spencer to find a place for themselves as queers in a straight world, and they all acknowledge the role Spectrum has played in bolstering their self-confidence. As Ditto says about her first visit to the space,

> Then I got to go and see there was all these people and I wasn't a freak; I wasn't that one person who's that gender they don't know. I was Ditto and everyone was okay with that. So "I'm like, oh yeah, I'm bi!" "That's cool, I'm a lesbian! What, you want a cookie for that?" It didn't feel like it was a judge thing, it was like, that's cool, it was like saying, "Oh by the way, I live here." It was not a big thing.

This does not, however, change the fact that people whose gender expression confounds a clearly male or female attribution shoulder the burden of society's discomfort with gender ambiguity. Adolescent negotiation of sexual and gender identities is not a universal experience. It is still the case that those young people who are consciously forming sexual and gender identities are members of already queer communities, while most teenagers who conform to the dominant order take their sexuality and gender for granted.

In his discussion of the state's role in "administering gender," the legal scholar Dean Spade shows how identity documentation, sex-segregated facilities, and access to healthcare are all ways that the government plays a role in upholding binary gender norms, a role that he argues results in violence against trans* and genderqueer people. Spade states that "data collection and management-focused programs like driver's licensing, Social Security benefits, and taxation are less often analyzed for their racist and sexist impacts. In reality, these systems are part of a national security project that constructs national norms to sort populations for the distribution of life chances."[27] Because the state does not permit for gender neutrality or gender ambiguity, efforts towards trans* rights have had to focus on formal recognition within institutions that control driver's licenses, passports, and other forms of formal identification, requiring rights to access medical and surgical care in order to transition from one gender to another.[28] The effort to "prove" one's binary gender spills over quite significantly into the debate over sex-segregated facilities, like bathrooms.

The increasing visibility of trans* children in schools has erupted in countless debates over bathroom use. Parents, administrators, and teachers battle over whether a child has a right to use the gendered/sexed bathroom of their choice, while the simplest solution—gender neutral bathrooms—rarely comes up. And given that people whose gender seems to deviate from the norm are assumed to be sexual deviants, particularly in the case of transwomen, adult anxieties about bathroom use are deeply tied to adult anxieties about sexuality.[29]

As advocacy for the legislation of trans* rights has increased, the opposition has resulted in the form of what Kristen Schilt and Laurel Westbrook call "penis panics."[30] By conflating transwomen with sexual predators, campaigns that oppose trans* rights legislation work to convince people that allowing male bodies into women's sex-segregated spaces will result in increased incidence of sexual assault. In addition to reducing all women and girls to vulnerable victims and all men and boys to sexual predators, this discourse relies on an essentialist understanding of sex, where genitals are the sole determination of one's gender. North Carolina's 2016 House Bill 2, the Public Facilities Privacy and Security Act, legally defines sex as "the physical condition of being male or female, which is stated on a person's birth certificate."[31] It is considered by many to be one of the most—if not the most—anti-LGBTQ pieces of legislation passed in the United States to date, and it has resulted in widespread boycotts of North Carolina. The U.S. Department of Justice (under the Obama administration) considered House Bill 2 a violation of the Civil Rights Act, Title IX, and the Violence Against Women Act and as a result filed suit against the state of North Carolina and several entities within it.[32] Setting aside for a moment the notion that this type of legislation is hauntingly similar to Jim Crow–era "separate but equal" forms of racial segregation, there are other reasons that legislating gender in this way does not make sense. Although in some states it is possible to have the sex on one's birth certificate changed, the reality is that doing so requires access to a lot of resources, including medical diagnoses, hormonal treatments, and surgeries, along with the where-withal to navigate complicated bureaucracies. In addition, requiring that a person's gender expression and identity be in line with the sex on their birth certificate negates gender non-conformity and all the myriad ways people experience their gender. Not all trans* people desire to identify within the gender binary, and not all genderqueer people identify as trans*.

Allowing a transitioning child to use the gendered/sexed bathroom of their choice or a segregated bathroom within the school, as has so often been the case, does not solve the bathroom problem for people who embody ambiguous gender. There continue to be human bodies society struggles to categorize as "girl" or "boy." Bathrooms, security lines in airports, organized sports, and even identification checks for purchasing tobacco or alcohol become sites of struggle and, in some cases, violence for people whose gender is often mis-attributed. Beyond these day-to-day obstacles to moving around in society, genderqueer people are particularly susceptible to violence in the form of bullying and harassment, often because of the way their gender ambiguity fails to align their gender and sexuality. Trans* and genderqueer people have been violently attacked and/or murdered by perpetrators who justify their actions by accusing their victims of deception when their genitals do not align with their perceived gender.[33] Embodying ambiguous gender comes at a very high cost in our society.

I have tried to show here the strength of the binary gender order, which continues to compel people—whether they are trans*, gen-derqueer, or cisgender—to either be a boy or a girl, not something in between, and that the gender order is upheld through the process of external gender attribution, not just internal gender identity. Although Spectrum youth in many ways embrace gender ambiguity—like Gabe, for example, who says it makes him happy to be mistaken for a woman—Ditto is still seen as a freak, often identifiable as neither a man nor a woman. Jude, who identifies as a woman but is really most comfortable as an androgynous person, says, "I feel like it's a lot of pressure behind me to dress and act feminine, because I identify that way." Finally, while countless stories about trans* children and their parents fighting for the right to transition and be supported in their communities and schools is a sign of a revolution, the dominant message remains that one must still be a boy or a girl, not both or neither, which assumes that there is such a thing as a boy or a girl and that we all know who they are when we see them. What does that mean for Spencer, who after several years of rejecting his female self and identifying as a guy, needs the space and freedom to be a girl sometimes, too? In our efforts to protect transbinary youth, we need to take care not to create more invisible categories of people who will be marginalized in the process.[34] Perhaps another one of the ways society can break the habit of the gender binary will be through queer media, a topic I take up in the next chapter.

4

"Google Knows Everything"

Finding Queer Media

Aaron, his boyfriend Miguel, and their friend Alex started coming to Spectrum about three weeks ago. They always show up as a threesome, although sometimes they have Aaron's fifteen-year-old brother in tow. Aaron and Alex are nineteen years old, Miguel is twenty, and all identify as gay men. They are friendly and vibrant and have brought some new energy to the space in the midst of what had been feeling like a lull. They made friends with Travon right away, and for the past several afternoons, the group of them has met up to play Bullshit, the card game. Miguel and Alex are loud and outgoing, while Aaron's quiet confidence grounds the group.

One afternoon, not long after they started coming to Spectrum, Aaron approached me and asked if he could participate in an interview. We retreat to the medical clinic and talk for a little over an hour. Aaron is a freshman in college at the state's flagship university. As a Chicanx and a first-generation college student, he is one of an elite few to attend this school. This also makes him quite an outlier within the Spectrum community as very few of the college-aged youth are attending college at all, far less attending a school of this status. He grew up in a rural part of the state, raised for most of his childhood by a young single mother, as his father had been incarcerated. He and his mother lived at times with his grandparents, who, along with his mother, have been strong sources of support and love in his life. His mother eventually remarried and had children with Aaron's stepfather. They live in the northern suburbs now.

Aaron is a film buff who aspires to be an independent filmmaker, so we swapped stories about some of our favorite filmmakers, like Robert Rodriguez and Lars von Trier. When I asked him if he feels that film has influenced his sexuality, he described his experience seeing *Brokeback Mountain* for the first time. *Brokeback Mountain*, the 2005 Ang Lee film adaptation of the E. Annie Proulx novella, tells a universal love story through the experience of two men in a secret relationship with each other. This R-rated movie includes scenes of sexual intimacy, much like any love story drama about a straight couple. Remarkably, the mainstream popularity of the film resulted in it being nominated for and winning several Oscars. This film had a profound impact on Aaron, who described watching the film in secret in his home, where he had to make sure no one was around before he watched a film about gay cowboys:

> I was into movies, and then there was *Brokeback Mountain*. Everybody hears about that. Although at the time it was one of the first one that I . . . the first gay movie that I had ever seen. And not only like . . . I don't know. I guess that not only did it help me be a little more comfortable with myself—with my sense of self—but um, I guess that kind of opened the world to other . . . other films. But I think that one in particular because there actually was, you know, a sex scene in that movie. And it was different for me. It's not like, um, I don't know. . . . I didn't watch it because I wanted to have—how would I say—be pleasured by that. But it was just different for me. You know like, I'd never seen something like that before.

Aaron explained that he had "seen a bunch of, you know, heterosexual [sex] scenes by that time and was familiar with the female body," but this was the first film he had seen that included sex between men that was not live-action pornography. Aaron's experience and his longing for a representation of a same-sex love story outside the realm of pornography demonstrates the important role media play in the sexual and romantic lives of young people. This chapter discusses how representations of queer orientations have proliferated in various media that are increasingly accessible to the youth of Spectrum and beyond. As media representations of same-sex sexuality and desire begin to proliferate, both within mainstream and alternative media, arguably most youth—not just those who are LGBTQ-identified—will have access to a new set of cultural scenarios that influence how they understand their sexuality. In other words, queer media are changing sexuality and gender for everyone.

Finding Queer Media Online

Something happened around the mid-1990s and into the middle of the first decade of the twenty-first century that forever changed the tide in favor of the queer: the internet. For the first time, people across the globe had simultaneous, instant access to cultural alternatives outside the mainstream. The internet and its access to global queer community and alternative culture is probably the most significant factor in the shifting norms around same-sex desire and LGBTQ culture for young people of this generation. Whereas previous LGBTQ-identified folks had to move to gay meccas like San Francisco, Chicago, and New York to find community, the internet provides instant community where queer culture can proliferate. In some of the earliest research done on the role of the internet on the LGBTQ rights movement, the psychobiologist James Weinrich found that "one of the most common benefits of the internet to the gay community . . . is that it permits geographically dispersed minority individuals to interact with one another as if they were a local majority."[1] The internet and internet communities have served as a positive source of sexuality information for sexual and gender minorities worldwide who seek an alternative to the derogatory and missing representations of themselves in mainstream media and formal sexuality education settings.[2] Notably, the sociologist C. J. Pascoe, in her research on young people using social media, found that, whereas straight-identified youth are distrustful of the internet as a way to meet friends and build community, almost the opposite is true for LGBTQ-identified youths, who depend on the internet as one of the few safe spaces they inhabit, where they can be open about their sexualities and gender and make friends with those who share their experiences.[3]

Among the youth of Spectrum, access to the internet appears ubiquitous. Within Spectrum itself there is access to a multitude of computers, all of which have internet access, and wireless within the building is accessible to anyone with a smartphone. Young people have smartphones or tablets of their own, including most of the working-class youth at Spectrum whose resources are quite restricted.

One of the ways that I encourage interviewees to talk to me about their self-understanding of their sexuality is by asking them to tell me about three things that they feel have most *influenced* their sexuality.

While such an open-ended question is admittedly subjective, it helps me to get a sense of the things external to the youths themselves that they consider important to who they are as sexual beings. It pushes them to consider the influence of the social on their sexuality, beyond simply the desires they experience internally. The five most common replies to this question, in descending order, are (1) some form of sexually explicit content (SEC) via media, (2) intimate relationships, (3) family influence or family members, 4) friends and peers, and 5) sexuality education (namely at Spectrum as opposed to school, where sexuality education is notoriously lacking). While interaction with other people—whether family, friends, or intimates—is clearly recognized as important by these young people, they claim that media—the internet in particular—is the most significant.

It is not surprising that some form of SEC via media is most frequently named as influential to the youths' sexuality.[4] Digital natives, those individuals who were born during or after the widespread use of digital technologies, are growing up in the midst of unprecedented access to information via media.[5] The internet allows confidential, quick, and easy access to diverse, explicit sexual images.[6] A study exploring German adolescents and pornography by media scholars found that, "for most adolescents, pornography is the only accessible source of depictions of sexual behavior; pornography might thus be used by adolescents not only for sexual arousal but also to discover sexual behavior and explore their own sexual preferences."[7] As Fiona, a nineteen-year-old white woman who identifies as bisexual, shared with me when I asked her about watching pornography, "You know it's how I learned what I like to do when I was younger. Um, it's how you learn new things most of the time. You can look up these positions or whatever. Find out how to do it." Pornography viewing is quite common among the young people I spoke with and often informs much of what they know about sexuality.

The youth of Spectrum, and likely a large number of their peers, know exactly where to go on the internet to look up SEC. They speak very matter-of-factly about the internet, and especially Google, as an obvious resource. They are not typically shy or embarrassed to tell me about their online explorations and approach the topic with the assumption that everyone does it. The following quotes from a variety of participants—including youths of various genders, sexual identities, and racial/ethnic groups—make evident the ease with which youth access SEC online through internet connections via computers and phones and easy-to-use search engines like Google:

> Especially our generation with the . . . the smart phones, and the internet, the wifi . . . all of that. It was simple.
> —Anthony, seventeen-year-old Latinx, identifies as gay

> I don't know. I wasn't originally like looking up porn, like, that's not how it started out. . . . I was on the computer, probably on some social website and something, and then I, like, I don't know, it just popped in my head and I got curious, so I searched. Like, if you want to know something what's the best way to find out? Go look [*laughs*]. So I did, and I found like, pictures and videos and I was like, "Oh!" [*laughs*].
> —Travon, sixteen-year-old Black male, identifies as queer

> MARY: So you looked at porn? Where did you find that? On the internet or in magazines? Or how did you find it?
> FIONA: Internet. Late at night when my parents weren't awake.
> MARY: Okay. And how did you discover that?
> FIONA: Just in Google, like, "naked people" or, I don't even know, like "boobs."
> —Fiona, nineteen-year-old white woman, identifies as bisexual

> MARY: Where would you go to find out information?
> NIK: Google. 'Cause unfortunate as it is, Google knows everything.
> —Nik, eighteen-year-old white man, identifies as gay

As these quotes demonstrate, accessing SEC on the internet is not a challenge for young people. Further, many of the youths share stories of accessing the internet and sexually explicit content in their homes with little trouble. Digital natives tend to be quite savvy when it comes to covering their tracks and in many cases are far more nimble on the internet than their parents or guardians, making it easy for them to discreetly access content that adults in their family might find questionable.[8] Although some of the youths shared stories about being caught looking at

SEC online, none of them said that their parents were using any sort of blockers or restrictions through their internet service.

It is significant to consider the profound shift that has taken place over the course of the last century when it comes to how young people become sexual. Prior to the proliferation of mainstream media, sexual subjectivity was formed largely within the family, church, and school. All three of these institutions are dominated by adults. But the ability adults have to control and influence the sexual formation of young people has shifted tremendously with the proliferation and availability of new media. And while the availability of media is not always liberating, it has expanded the available options and loosened tight social control over sexuality. Although mainstream media continues to be largely heteronormative and homophobic in nature, LGBTQ-identified youth have access to an unprecedented amount of alternative media—including self-produced media—in which representations of queer sexualities and genders are proliferating. In particular, in this chapter I discuss Spectrum youths' interest in erotic *anime* and fan fiction as alternative forms of media. But first I discuss the importance of representation to the formation of sexual scripts and the history of widespread erasure and the stigma of homosexuality in mainstream media.

Cultural Scenarios and Sexual Scripts

Dramaturgical analysis is a useful tool for demystifying seemingly "natural" human conduct. In particular, the script and all its contingent parts—the writer, the producer, the actor, the set, the props, and the stage—are metaphors to help us recognize and notice the way that shared social understandings help members of a society successfully interact with each other day in and day out.[9] Scripts describe learned social behaviors that, when successfully deployed, are largely invisible in social interaction yet become obvious when there is a deviation or failed cue that calls for improvisation.

Sexual scripts describe learned, shared social understandings about what is and what is not sexual, as well as how to conduct oneself in a sexual interaction.[10] How is it that we are able to identify that something is sexual or not? How is it that we know how to behave sexually with another person or alone? John Gagnon, who along with William Simon developed sociological theories about sexual conduct using scripting theory in the 1970s, explains scripts this way: "Scripts [are] most often treated as heuristic devices to be used by observers to better interpret sexual conduct at three levels: cultural scenarios (such as pornography and the cinema), interpersonal interactions (as in specific sexual acts), and intrapsychic processes (e.g., sexual fantasies, plans, remembrances)."[11] Sexual scripting theory argues that biology is a weak explanation for sexuality and that, in fact, much of what we think we know about sex and sexuality is learned behavior, not instinctual. We have to be taught and learn what sexual is (and is not) and how to engage in sex. Scripting theory makes this learning more visible.

Cultural scenarios, as one component of sexual scripts, are what help us to determine the difference between a prostrate or pelvic exam at the doctor's office and a sexual encounter with a lover, where the former is not meant to arouse us sexually while the latter is. Cultural scenarios teach the (non-)sexual script in many different ways. Children learn from adults and peers how to follow the sexual script and pay attention to cues. In U.S. culture, it is the norm to teach children that certain parts of their body are private and should be kept to themselves. For example, most children are taught, one way or another, not to touch their penises or vulvas in public. This might be one of the earliest moments of learning the sexual script, as children learn that something about their sex organs is different from other parts of their body. While the example I've used here is quite simple, imagine all of the ways that people are taught from family members, authority figures, and peers how their bodies are (non-)sexual. Scripting theory can help make this process visible.

Beyond family, friends, and other adults, cultural scenarios are learned through various media, including television, film, books, comics, songs, art, and social media. Society learns what is culturally appropriate through media, which in the United States relentlessly demonstrates a dominant narrative about sexuality that is heterosexual, male-centered, penile-to-vaginal, and largely monogamous. While there are certainly alternatives to this dominant cultural scenario, many of the intimate, sexual relations portrayed through media are incredibly monotonous in their portrayal of human sexuality. Of particular interest here is the rampant heterosexuality portrayed in the media. This does not mean that alternative scripts are not available, but when it comes to mainstream media and sexuality, heterosexual pairings rule the day. But heterosexual scripts are not fixed, and as society's notions of appropriate sexuality has shifted, the dominant scripts have changed, too. For example, while still largely heterosexual in nature, it is more common to see sex scenes on television or in film that ostensibly focus more on women's pleasure, like an increase in scenes where men perform oral sex on women.

In many ways, cultural scenarios via media can be helpful tools for novices who are just learning about sexuality, yet they can also stifle creativity when it comes to sexual behavior because they may limit one's notion of what's possible or acceptable when it comes to sexual conduct. In his discussion of how sexual scripts influence gender preference, Gagnon stresses that people experience "changes in gender preference in erotic relations" across the course of their lives. But he points out that this instability is particularly common among adolescents "when gender-appropriate sexual scripts are in the process of acquisition."[12] Children and adolescents typically have had less access to a diversity of scripts because of various institutionalized forms of control through family, religion, school, and restricted access to media. Too often they are shielded from a potentially diverse array of sexual cultural scenarios that inform their scripts. At the same time, they are still new to sexuality and not yet socialized into heteronormative sexualities in the same ways that adults may be.

In his critique of using scripting theory to explain sexuality, Jonathan Green argues that sociologists are guilty of relying too much on the social to understand sexuality, and not enough on the subconscious or psychoanalytic. He argues that, in addition to cultural scenarios and interpersonal interactions, both of which can be observed empirically, the intrapsychic processes are influenced by an erotic habitus that is formed largely in our subconscious but influenced by the social. He urges sociologists to consider that, "stretched into an all-purpose, one-size-fits-all framework," scripting theory fails to adequately explain sexual desire.[13] "Indeed, a 'script' is not a master status, nor a social structure, nor an unconscious, psychic structure. Scripting processes are, however, relevant to how these elements bear on what we do sexually and with whom."[14] Therefore, keeping in mind that the media we consume does not predetermine our sexual desires and sexual subjectivities, the cultural scenarios youth encounter through media provide a plethora of examples with which to explore how young people do learn *something* about sexual conduct. Given one's sexual habitus, in particular one that is queerly oriented, the absence or presence of same-sex desire and homosexuality provided via cultural scenarios is important to consider.

In a society in which same-sex erotic desire has been intentionally censored from the mainstream media (which I discuss at more length below), same-sex sexual scripts are acquired largely outside the mainstream. For example, scripts might be learned within a community of peers, like an LGBTQ center. When it comes to alternative media, same-sex sexual scripts abound in various sources on the internet, including pornography and social media, along with other forms of media like foreign film, novels, and poetry.

Therefore in the United States there is a lack of mainstream cultural scenarios that represent same-sex desire. It becomes clear within this study that the youth of Spectrum value same-sex and genderqueer cultural scenarios that they discover outside mainstream media. Arguably, as the normalization of homosexuality increases in U.S. culture, so has the quantity of representations of same-sex desire. This has implications not only for those who claim LGBTQ-identities and experience same-sex desire but also for the increasing acceptance of sexual and gender fluidity among all sorts of people. Compared to a previous generation of LGBTQ-identified people, who had to seek out community in bars, clubs, and other public places where gay people congregated, Spectrum youth have access to a global community via the internet and, therefore, a multitude of cultural scenarios that represent same-sex desire. In the coming decade, we are likely to see a mainstreaming of same-sex sexual scripts and cultural scenarios that will permanently change the sexual landscape of our culture.

Missing and Misrepresented on Screen

The twentieth-century censoring of U.S. media—film, television, and print—resulted in a cultural erasure of homosexuality.[15] This, along with the medical and psychological professions' past (and in some cases ongoing) treatment of gayness as something to eliminate, rather than affirm, has contributed to a deeply homophobic and transphobic U.S. culture that we are still contending with today.[16] In the context of such powerful social control, the battle for LGBTQ rights has been difficult. While the movement has recently been wildly successful at combating institutionalized transphobia and homophobia, including the reversal of legislation like the Defense of Marriage Act (DOMA) and Don't Ask Don't Tell (DADT), along with other major legislative and legal wins, U.S. mainstream culture continues to marginalize representations of LGBTQ lives.

The 1915 Supreme Court case *Mutual Film Corporation v. Industrial Commission of Ohio* ruled that the film industry—determined to be a for-profit entertainment product as opposed to a member of the press—should not be protected by First Amendment freedom-of-speech rights, leaving the film industry vulnerable to censorship. Vito Russo's extensive history of representations of homosexuality in the U.S. film industry, *The Celluloid Closet*, explains that "by 1922 there were censorship bills before the legislatures of thirty-two states, and throughout the nation the distinct odor of moral indignation was rising at an industry that at times seemed to embody wicked behavior of all sorts."[17] Homosexuality, as a form of deviant sexuality, was a censored topic in all of the various statutes. While not specifically forbidden, "cross dressing, weakness in men, and over-intellectualism were sometimes direct statements about deviant sexuality," meaning that characters associated with the sissy were associated with homosexuality and therefore also subject to censorship.[18]

In addition to the state censorship statutes, the creation of the Motion Picture Production Code in 1930 (and similarly the Code of Practices for Television Broadcasters in 1951) had a profound impact on the lack of representations of homosexuality in film in the United States. The role of the Code and the office that administered it was to anticipate censorship before it happened and therefore was a form of self-regulation for the film industry. Often referred to as the Hays Office (after Will H. Hays, who led the Motion Picture Producers and Distributers of America from 1922 to 1945), this self-censoring body ensured that films coming out of Hollywood were in line with Christian—specifically Catholic—morals and values. In addition to forbidding nudity (even in silhouette) and sex perversion (homosexuality being among the perversions), the Code forbade representations of miscegenation, the illegal traffic of drugs, white slavery, and ridicule of the clergy, among other things. Thanks to the

Code and various censorship statutes across the country, representations of queerness or homosexuality, save for the most metaphorical, were successfully removed from mainstream media in the United States. The Code was enforced within the U.S. film industry beginning in the 1930s and continued through 1968, when the Motion Picture Association of America film rating system went into effect.[19]

Decades prior to the censoring of the film and television industries, the Act for the Suppression of Trade in, and Circulation of, Obscene Literature and Articles of Immoral Use, commonly known as the Comstock Act, also had an important impact on the repression of homosexuality and other forms of "perverse" sexuality. The Comstock Act, passed in 1873, made it illegal to send obscene materials like erotica, abortifacients, birth control, sex toys, personal letters alluding to sexual content or information, or any information about the above-mentioned items through the U.S. Postal Service. Combined, the censorship statutes, the film and television industry's self-regulation of content, and the Comstock Act effectively removed representations of same-sex desire and any notion of the homosexual from the mainstream media. This kind of censorship contributed to the formation of a transphobic and homophobic culture, taking a destructive toll on sexual and gender minorities.

A growing secularism and rejection of conservative cultural norms saw the relaxation of censorship measures in the 1960s and 1970s. In part, control of the media became less realistic as the culture globalized and technology advanced, making it impossible to censor all media. For example, foreign films that portrayed complex characters and stories with homosexual content made their way to U.S. theaters. Further, in 1952 the U.S. Supreme Court had overturned its previous decision that films were not subject to First Amendment rights, which opened the door to more freedom of content.[20]

As the Code was slowly abandoned, representations of queerness began to surface more and more in U.S. films, but too often the narratives told were pathologizing. LGBTQ characters were portrayed as dangerous serial killers, like Jame Gumb, aka "Buffalo Bill," in *Silence of the Lambs*,[21] or as damaged individuals whose lives end in tragedy. According to Russo, "In twenty-two of twenty-eight films dealing with gay subjects from 1962 to 1978, major gay characters onscreen ended in suicide or violent death."[22] When gay/trans people weren't represented as pathological, they often filled the role of comic relief. Even though the gay rights movement was in full swing and various industries were paying attention to what they saw as a new market, the film industry continued to rely on old tropes. This legacy continues to this day, where LGBTQ-identified characters have proliferated but whose storylines are still commonly written as tragic, dysfunctional, and outside the norm. For example, in *Brokeback Mountain*, Ennis learns from his lover Jack's wife that Jack was killed in an accident changing a tire, yet Ennis then imagines Jack being beaten to death by thugs with a tire iron, leaving the viewer with the distinct impression that Jack was killed for being queer.

Since Russo first published *The Celluloid Closet* in 1981, the treatment of gay, lesbian, bisexual, and transgender characters and lives in film has changed considerably. Elimination of the Code, the progression of the LGBTQ rights movement, and shifting mores have resulted in an increase in films that deal more honestly with homosexuality and gender non-conformance. Yet many of the sensitive, complex stories are told through independent and foreign film, while mainstream Hollywood blockbusters continue to be unapologetically homophobic. Further, among those mainstream blockbuster films and television shows that do feature LGBTQ characters, they tend to reinforce hegemonic masculinity and heteronormativity.[23]

During the late 1990s, when the youth of Spectrum were children, there were few representations in mainstream media of healthy gay or transgender people or of same-sex desire. The tide began to change when, in 1997, Ellen DeGeneres came out as lesbian on national TV and, in 1998, *Will & Grace*, a sitcom featuring a successful, healthy, happy gay lead, began airing. While incredibly important icons in the cultural representation of gay people as complex characters, neither Ellen nor Will (the gay male lead in *Will & Grace*) are necessarily bastions of queerness. Too often, gay characters and celebrities who are most palatable to an ostensibly straight viewing audience are the ones who get the most screen time.[24]

A string of significant U.S. television shows and films were produced in the late twentieth and early twenty-first century that featured complex gay characters, breaking the spell of dangerous, broken, or absurd LGBTQ stereotypes. These include *Philadelphia* (1993), *The Bird Cage* (1996), *Queer as Folk* (2000–2005), *Six Feet Under* (2001–2005), and

The L Word (2004–2006), but much of these were geared toward adult audiences and are less accessible to young people. Television shows for teenagers with LGBTQ-identified characters—including *Buffy the Vampire Slayer* (1997–2003), *Dawson's Creek* (1998–2003), and *Felicity* (1998–2002)—have had an important influence on the young people who grew up watching them, of course, but they are exceptions, not the rule. Depictions of healthy, average, regular LGBTQ *children* or *teenage* characters on television or in the movies have been essentially nonexistent until the last decade.

Children in U.S. society are largely framed as sexual innocents, therefore acknowledging a child character's sexuality is quite outside the norm. Yet, as culture scholars like Jack Halberstam have pointed out, while it may not specifically refer to sexuality, children's programming is known for being rather queer. In the book *Gaga Feminism*, Halberstam praises the animated show *SpongeBob SquarePants* (1999–present)—and others like it—for transgressing gender norms: "While earlier generations of boys and girls were raised on cartoon worlds populated by cats and mice, dogs and rabbits chasing each other across various domestic landscapes, this generation has come of age to an animated mythological universe populated by characters with eccentric and often simply weird relations to gender."[25] *SpongeBob SquarePants*, a favorite among the youth of Spectrum, is a recognizably queer character in definitively straight pop culture.

Teenagers are more often framed in popular culture as having a sexuality, therefore one would think that, throughout the 1980s, 1990s, and 2000s, more television shows and movies portraying gay teenagers would have been produced. Despite the recent increase of LGBTQ characters in mainstream media marketed to adolescents (most of which were just coming on the air as I encountered Spectrum)—including popular television shows like *Supernatural* (2005–present), *Doctor Who* (2005–present), *Glee* (2009–2015), *RuPaul's Drag Race* (2009–present), *Teen Wolf* (2011–present), *The Fosters* (2013–present), and *Sean Saves the World* (2013–2014)—most characters and narratives continue to perpetuate a heteronormative world view. Same-sex attractions, behaviors, and relationships depicted in mainstream media as normal, healthy, developmentally appropriate human behavior continue to be the exception to the rule.

Half a century of social justice activism on the part of the transgender and LGB community has still only more recently succeeded in a significant increase in acceptability of media representation of members of these communities. But it has also resulted in an alternative cultural explosion, in which those whose representations are missing or distorted create their own cultural representations. Many of the young people of Spectrum, when asked what has influenced their sexuality, rarely, if ever, referred to any sort of mainstream media as a source of reliable representations of gender, sexuality, romance, and intimacy. Rather, a few described the lack of stories or representations of individuals with same-sex desires in the media.

Jack, an eighteen-year-old, white transman who identifies as pansexual but "leaning towards gay," explains that, in fact, his lack of access to cultural scenarios that accurately represented his experience meant that he had the opportunity to develop his own authentic sexuality. He wanted information about how to be in a same-sex and/or genderqueer relationship but could not find those representations easily:

> It was kind of the lack of those things that I think I got to come up with a more authentic, what's "good for me" thing. . . . The lack of specifics being part of it, but then also in terms of this idea of how various relationships develop and such that was something that, you know, [*pause*] first of all, your major media has one kind of fairy-tale view to it which I never really bought into that much because none of the major media fairy-tale stories every really worked out for me.

Through Spectrum, peers, and the internet, while young people were in the process of discovering their sexuality, they were also discovering queer media and finding a place for themselves within it.

Anime and Fan Fiction

A number of Spectrum youths mention their interest in *anime*—Japanese animation—and *manga*—Japanese graphic novels, as having been significant influences on their sexuality. *Anime* is animated storytelling, similar to cartoons in the United States. But *anime* differs from cartoons because in the United States cartoons are largely associated with children's programming, while *anime* in Japan and other East Asian countries is produced for audiences of differing ages, encompassing a wide variety of genres.[26] *Anime*, a wildly popular genre of media in Japanese culture, first came to U.S. television in the 1960s but really saw broad exposure in a wave of licensing and distribution in the United States in the mid-1990s. *Anime* shows were broadcast in the United States with English subtitles or dubbing, but otherwise they were left unchanged from their original versions, resulting in a curious unintended consequence.

Given that gender and sexuality are social constructions, meaning that gender norms and roles considered appropriate in the United States might differ from those of another country or culture, Japanese animation featured characters that appeared notably queer to a U.S. audience.[27] Gender-bending characters who show affection and intimacy for characters that appear to be of the same-sex are normal in many *anime* stories. This is a reflection of Japan's own social constructions of gender and sexuality, where homosexuality is not criminalized to the same extent, nor is sexual orientation a strong marker of identity. Therefore, art created in a culture that is more tolerant of queer gender and homosexuality may appear queer through a U.S.-centric lens.[28]

Many of the Spectrum youths mentioned first being exposed to *anime* as young kids through *Sailor Moon*, a Japanese *anime* show that began airing as an English-dubbed version on network television in the United States in 1995 on Fox and the WB networks and later, in 1998, on Cartoon Network's *anime* show *Toonami*.[29] As an example of queer gender and homosexuality, *Sailor Moon* features a character called Haruka or Sailor Uranus. Haruka, a female character who was often androgynous in appearance, if not outright masculine at times, shares an intimate relationship with another female character, Michiru, or Sailor Neptune. Although the show's original creators have acknowledged Sailor Uranus and Sailor Neptune as a same-sex intimate pairing, in a perhaps ill-fated attempt to erase their lesbianism, the two were made out to be cousins in the U.S. English-dubbed version of the show, albeit cousins who kissed, held hands, and competed in and won an "affection contest."[30]

Another example, *Ranma ½* (pronounced "Ranma One Half"), was released on video in the United States in 1989. This popular *anime* features a boy named Ranma who is cursed when he falls into an ancient well. As a result, whenever he encounters cold water, he turns into a girl version of himself, and when he encounters hot water, he returns to his boy self. Beyond the gender bending that is inherent to the show's overarching plotline, there are various minor plotlines that raise the specter of queer sexuality when, for example, Ranma's enemy, Tatewaki, another boy, falls in love with Ranma's girl self.

Released on DVD in 2008 and airing on the Funimation cable network starting in 2009, *Ouran High School Host Club* is the story of a high school version of a host club, a type of bar that is popular in East Asia where men (hosts) cater to the needs of their female clients as a form of entertainment.[31] In this *anime*, the hosts are male students who wait on the privileged female students of Ouran High. When a new girl student, Haruhi Fujioka, stumbles into the Host Club and accidentally breaks a ridiculously expensive vase, the boys of the host club, mistaking her for male because of her androgynous appearance, give her the option to work off what she owes for the broken vase. In addition to Haruhi's gender-bending role, the show includes a set of boy twin hosts who, in a homoerotic narcissistic twist, appear to be in love with each other. And Haruhi's father, Ryoji, is a professional cross-dresser, who works in a host bar himself.

These are just three examples of *anime* the youth of Spectrum identified to me as having queer characters and plot lines. These descriptions should not be confused for a critical cultural analysis of *anime*. Rather, I've given very brief synopses here in order to give readers unfamiliar with gender-bending and same-sex intimacy tropes in *anime* a sense of what it can look like. Debates about the various queer interpretations made about these shows exist among true fans and experts of *anime* and *manga* and are widely accessible on fan wikis, blogs, and publications. More important to my analysis is the point that, in a U.S. media culture where same-sex intimacy and queer gender has been largely suppressed, particularly in programming marketed to kids, *anime*'s representation of gender fluidity and negotiation of shifting norms around sexuality speak particularly strongly to the youth of Spectrum.

When I asked Zia—who is nineteen years old, Black, and identifies as queer—to name three things that most influenced her sexuality, she explained why *Sailor Moon* was one:

Hmmmm. Let's see [*pause*]. *Sailor Moon*? [*laughs*]. Yes, 'cause there's this one character . . . she's just so beautiful and so magical and so hot. And like, when I saw her I was just young, I was young when I was watching *Sailor Moon*. . . . She was the outcast, but she was very mysterious. Which made me just really attracted to her. . . . But she just had a very defining look and, like, a very mysterious and, like, alluring personality, which just like made me super attracted to her. Plus her . . . fighting partners were lesbians, so I was just like, when Sailor Uranus came on I was like, Is that a guy or a girl? It's like, it don't matter, they're all hot.

Ditto, a twenty-year-old bisexual, biracial Latinx, described a similar connection with the queer, gender-bending characters in *Sailor Moon*:

The wonderful thing about that, they were like, "This person is gay and this person is cross-dressing and this person is doing this and this person is now transgender." Even in *Sailor Moon*, the Japanese version had sequences where, like, full guy characters, looked like a guy, act like a guy, would transform into a chick, and it was like, it was not a big thing. Yeah, that thing, and it just does that, it just happens. They walked down the street and walked around the corner, that's how casual it was. So connecting that with me coming out was like, yeah, walk down the street round the corner, it was the casual flow through, which was really nice.

Gabe, an eighteen-year-old genderqueer Latinx who identifies as bisexual, explains here how his childhood impression of a gender-bending character in one of his favorite *animes*, *InuYasha*, changed as he got older and became more aware of queer sexuality and gender:

The main . . . homosexual character that's blatantly obvious, but I was not aware of when I was thirteen, was . . . Jakotsu who, he is a mercenary who works with this . . . with this band of seven brothers. And um, he's very flamboyant. Looks like a woman. Has lipstick on. Wears a female kimono and I had no idea . . . like, the whole time—when I was thirteen through fifteen—I thought it was just a girl pretending to be a guy. And then it wasn't until I hit sixteen and I was watching the series over again, it got near the end and Jakotsu came on and I'm like, "Wait a minute."

The character Gabe refers to, Jakotsu, is described on the *Inu Ya-sha* website as "a stereotypically flamboyant homosexual; examples of which would be his admiration of Kōga's loincloth, his advances towards Miroku and Inuyasha upon meeting them, and his admiration of Sesshōmaru's appearance during battle."[32]

Not all of the youths I encountered referenced *anime* specifically as one of the things that influenced their sexuality, but most, if not all, Spectrum youth are familiar with *anime*, associating it as part of queer culture. For example, in a conversation I had with César, Spectrum's program director, he explained how gay kids and *anime* fans often intersect. While he was in high school, members of the Gay-Straight Alliance and members of the *Anime* Club were often the same people. *Anime*, as a component of nerd culture in the United States, has long been associated with outsider, or queer, status.

While *Sailor Moon* and other cartoons like it may have been the youths' first exposure to *anime*, once introduced to the genre, the internet opened up an entire world of access to *anime* as queer culture. The youths quickly discovered that the seemingly deviant gender and sexuality norms portrayed in *Sailor Moon* were common in *anime* from Japan. Susan Napier describes a characteristic of *anime* as the "mode of the festival . . . for a brief moment norms are transgressed or actually inverted. The weak hold power, sexual and gender rules are broken or reversed, and a state of manic intensity replaces conventional restraint."[33] In the United States, cartoons have typically been considered children's entertainment. In Japan, *anime* is not just for children, but for people of all ages, and in fact, various forms of erotic-themed *anime* (cartoons and comics) exist and are accessible to just about anyone with internet access.

There are several different genres of erotic *anime*. Each genre represents a different sexual preference, orientation, or fetish. For example, the most commonly discussed among the youth of Spectrum were *yaoi* and *yuri*, boys' love and girls' love, respectively. Both of these genres, which tell stories of same-sex attraction, romance, and intimacy, appeal to fans of all genders.[34] Adam, an eighteen-year-old white man who identifies as gay, told me of his early fascination with *Sailor Moon* and how later he discovered *anime* erotica and the profound impact it had on him:

Gay *anime* was such a . . . breakthrough, I guess, because . . . I don't even know how I even started watching it, or how it came about. . . . It was during seventh grade going to eighth grade. And I started watching—I don't even know how I got to it—I think I was watching regular porn, and then I saw a link or something and it was like, "Oh, what's this?" And it was two guys and I was like, "Oh, what the fuck?" And then I was like, "Oh, let's explore this." I think that's how . . . I think that's what happened. . . . So to just see like, two super hot *anime* guys like, liking each other, and going at it with each other was like, "Oh, this is hot." That's just . . . oh, that's so appealing to me. And I couldn't understand why at the time and I didn't know what it meant at the time, but I just knew that secretly I would have . . . I would like, find it when everyone was asleep or everyone was out of the house, I'd watch it. And I was like, "Oh this is . . . this is my shit." And I'd just watch that same *anime* over and over and over.

Isaac, a nineteen-year-old who identifies as gay and male, has a white father and a Black mother. He has a warm, gap-toothed smile with eyes so dark they are almost black. His soft, tightly curled hair is generally kept short. He tends to dress in dark clothes and often covers his head in a hoodie. Isaac is an artist and an introvert who speaks at a slow, measured pace in a deep tone. He first came to Spectrum when he was seventeen, and the summer I interviewed him, he had been showing up just about every day. A huge fan of all things Japanese, Isaac helped me to understand the varying degrees of intimacy portrayed in *manga* and *anime*:

Yeah, *yaoi* and *yuri*, um, they range 'cause some of them are more intense. And some of them are very light. Like the ones I found I actually found at a Barnes & Noble [bookstore]. So they have really toned down the ones in public, but if you're looking for ones that are a little more deep into the sex and the sexual intercourse, you would most likely be able to find that online or just read it on online websites that people post that whole thing on.

Both Adam's and Isaac's comments suggest that erotic *anime* is one form of alternative media where LGBTQ youth are discovering cultural scenarios that represent homosexual sex and queerness. I discuss boys' love in *anime*, or *yaoi*, and its impact on queer culture, in more detail below.

Another form of queer culture popular among the youth of Spectrum is fan fiction. Fan fiction writers expand on popular literary canon, like the *Harry Potter* series,[35] for example, by reimagining the characters and storylines to suit their own creative impulses. Typically, fan fiction is shared among a community of fans, both readers and writers, not sold or published in print. The education scholar Rebecca Black recognizes in fan fiction "the many ways in which fans are taking up elements of pop culture and then redistributing them in new forms that are imbued with meanings that are grounded in the lived realities and social worlds of fans."[36] Although fan fiction is not necessarily a new phenomenon, it has grown in popularity aided largely by the internet, which fosters an enormous community of amateur writers and their reading publics. Creators and readers of fan fiction flock to various webpages and social media sites to reimagine their favorite characters from *Harry Potter*, *Twilight*, *The Hunger Games*, and more.[37] Like *anime*, fan fiction is associated with fandom and nerd-dom; it has largely existed outside the cultural mainstream as a site of queerness. Isaac, who not only reads fan fiction but authors it, explains the important role fan fiction plays in the lives of youths who are often misunderstood and misrepresented in mainstream media:

> I just believe . . . considering when you're a teenager, finding the things that relate to you is really hard to do. So I just figure if I take characters that possibly a lot of people are familiar with, and actually associate with, and relate to . . . reading about them going through possibly a similar association that you're going through is something that they can really do and be something really enjoyable for them to read.

The internet greatly facilitates the distribution of fan fiction, although sharing fan fiction online is not a necessary component of the process. Red, a white twenty-year-old who identifies his gender as male and sexuality as "other," discovered Spectrum about two years ago by googling "LGBT center" right after moving here from a rural community in another state. Red is a husky kid with dark brown hair cut short up around his ears and neck. He has sideburns, long eyelashes, and a kind smile. Red loves *Buffy the Vampire Slayer*, singing karaoke, and performing in the monthly drag show. His was also the first interview I did in which *yaoi manga* came up. He described *yaoi* as a form of erotic *manga* that is popular among gay men in Japan. He was first exposed to it when a friend received one as a Christmas gift. He told me that he and two friends were involved in collaborative role-play in which they lived out their sexual fantasies by writing *yaoi* stories. Each of them plays a character in the story and writes that character's part. The three swap the book around at school, taking turns with it to add their part. Although none of them were sexually experienced, Red explained that by living vicariously through these characters, they gained a certain amount of sexual experience.

Fan fiction is an outlet for creating stories and cultural scenarios that are too often missing from mainstream discourses about sexuality and gender. By reading and writing fan fiction, LGBTQ youth can reimagine characters in their favorite movies and television shows as being more like them by writing in same-sex desires and relationships or non-normative embodiments of gender among characters. By sharing their stories and reading the fan fiction of others online, as well as co-writing stories with their peers, the youth are creating a network of information about what sex and relationships can look like outside of mainstream cultural scenarios.

The Queer Story of Slash Fan Fiction and *Yaoi Anime*

Long before the youth of Spectrum discovered *Harry Potter* fan fiction and *Sailor Moon anime*, two significant queer cultural phenomena had begun to occur almost simultaneously in the United States and Japan, testaments to the lack of representation of same-sex desires and gender non-conformity in mainstream media. Slash fan fiction in the United States and *yaoi manga* and *anime* in Japan are both forms of amateur art in which fans of popular media—television shows and movies in the United States and popular *manga* and *anime* series in Japan—rewrite leading male characters into same-sex romantic and sexual encounters. Both slash and *yaoi* developed during the 1970s, were created by women for a largely female audience, and were produced and shared via low-budget zines.

The term "slash" originates from the joining of two characters names by a backslash (/) to signify a story about their sexual pairing. For example, one of the first and perhaps most well-known slash pairings is between Captain Kirk and Mr. Spock of *Star Trek*, titled *K/S*. Similarly, *yaoi* artists paired ostensibly straight male characters from Japan's most popular *anime* shows, portrayed as young, somewhat androgynous "beautiful boys." *Yaoi* is also sometimes referred to as boys' love (BL) *manga/anime*. Both forms of fan fiction, slash and *yaoi*, allow individuals who are fans of particular stories to reimagine storylines and character development, often with the goal of countering masculinist, sexist plots and storylines in mainstream media. Matt Thorn, who writes about the Japanese amateur comics scene, describes slash and *yaoi* creators and their readers as queer: "In a sense the two genres mirror each other and speak to the desires of those who by choice or circumstance, do not fit neatly into society's prescribed norms of gender and sexuality. They do not see themselves as the conventionally beautiful characters who inevitably get the perfect guy or girl in mainstream media for women or men."[38] Both slash and *yaoi* were outlets for women to contribute to the culture of the sexual imaginary as subjects, an imaginary they had been largely left out of because of the objectification of women in mainstream culture. Interestingly, in both Japan and the United States, virtually simultaneously, these women artists chose to explore sexuality through male-male sexual encounters, queering the hegemonic norm.

Although there are differences between these two phenomena, the role they play as tools of counterhegemonic discourse, particularly related to sexuality and gender, cannot be overstated.[39] Speaking about slash, Henry Jenkins, a self-described "aca/fan"—someone who is an academic who studies popular culture as well as a fan of popular culture—was one of the first U.S. academics to talk about the counterhegemonic power of slash fiction. In his book *Textual Poachers: Television Fans and Participatory Culture*, he states that "slash . . . has many progressive elements: its development of more egalitarian forms of romantic and erotic relationships, its transcendence of rigidly defined categories of gender and sexual identity, [and] its critique of the more repressive aspects of traditional masculinity."[40] Matt Thorn expresses a similar sentiment on the subject of *yaoi*: "There can be little doubt that both the artists and the readers who are drawn to boys' love and *yaoi* are unhappy with mainstream norms of gender and sexuality."[41] By queering male and/or androgynous characters—as opposed to female—*yaoi* and slash creators could both avoid the male gaze that so frequently dominates representations of same-sex sexuality among women and play with the power that inherently comes with masculinity and maleness.

I encountered several youths at Spectrum who either read or wrote fan fiction and named it as a significant influence on their sexuality, namely because, within fan fiction, they were able to recognize and produce representations of themselves and their desires.

Rick is a nineteen-year-old white transman who identifies as demisexual. Today he's wearing a polo shirt, cargo shorts, and flip-flops. He wears glasses and his light-colored hair is buzzed short. He discovered Spectrum when he was fifteen, and now that he is away at college, he has stopped in over the summer to reconnect. A fast talker, Rick struggles with physical and mental disabilities that can be frustrating, but he is happier now that he is away at school and successfully passing as male most of the time. Rick claims, "Everything like, everything, before Spectrum, everything I knew from sex I learned about from lesbian fan fiction. Which is, it's good, it's well done, and I mean it's very accurate. . . . It's very well done."

Regardless of the "accuracy" of their representations of sexual conduct, for the youth of Spectrum, slash and *yaoi* are media in which queerness is represented in a way they can relate to. In her research on *yaoi* creators and readers, Akiko Mizoguchi, a visual and cultural studies expert, asserts that she is lesbian, in part, because of her love of *yaoi* as a young person. On being a reader of *yaoi* or BL, she claims that, "as I 'meet' these gay characters almost every week, I cannot help but think that the BL genre today is constantly holding a workshop, as it were, that pursues and experiments with case studies on gay-friendly society and gay citizens, even though the genre is mostly populated by heterosexual women."[42] Entire online communities have sprung up around various slash and *yaoi* stories and artists via internet chat rooms, social media like Tumblr, and websites that host authors' works.

Several decades ago, a relatively small group of women artists in the United States and Japan started a revolution producing "amateur" media as a form of resistance to dominant narratives in mainstream media. Now young people like those of Spectrum have access to an entire genre of queer culture produced by and for queer people in the form of slash and *yaoi*. As James Welker wrote in a *Signs* article where he explored the impact of *yaoi* on the sexual subjectivity and identity of its readers, "For readers whose experience of sexuality and gender contravenes hetero-normativity, works like *Song* and *Thomas* [early 1970s-era *yaoi* works] offer narrative safe havens where they can experiment with identity, find affirmation, and develop the strength necessary to find others like themselves and a sense of belonging."[43] Queer media like *anime* and fan fiction not only give queer-oriented youth a sense of belonging, they have the potential to shift norms across dominant culture, as well.

Queering Sexual Scripts

Cultural scenarios play a key part in the process of adopting sexual scripts. While sexual scripts are not what make us sexual per se, they are how we learn the difference between what is and is not sexual, allowing us to interact with each other in a meaningful way. Cultural scenarios, whether coming from parents, peers, or media, are situated in what is culturally appropriate; they reflect the hegemonic norms of a society, including norms that reflect the dominant gender order, among other things. Homosexuality, as a form of sexuality that was deemed deviant and morally offensive by moral entrepreneurs of the early twentieth century, was, through a complicated process of social control, effectively rendered perverse and unnatural. The censorship of the media that took place during the mid-twentieth century attempted to control cultural scenarios, demonizing any sexuality that was not heterosexual, reproductive, and monogamous.

Young people coming of age who identify with homosexuality and queerness during the rise of the internet have access to a wealth of alternatives to the mainstream and are building community in a different way than those who came before them. Whereas LGBTQ and/or queer culture was more geographically situated before, the internet has the potential to shift geographical boundaries and gives anyone with access to a computing device and the internet almost immediate connection to community. Even though mainstream media continue to be homophobic, the vestiges of censorship and social control that lingered in mainstream media are less influential in online content. Therefore young people today can, with perhaps more ease, access information, images, and cultural scenarios that include homosexual sex and queer community and culture.

Not long before the internet became available, resistance to hegemonic narratives in mainstream media had already begun as a result of various civil rights movements, including feminism and LGBTQ rights. By way of example, I explored how women artists who were fans of particular mainstream media literary narratives reconfigured the stories and characters of those stories to better represent their own (the women's) lived experiences. In a sexist and homophobic culture that objectified women's sexuality and pathologized homosexuality, these artists were able to create their own culture as a form of resistance. Slash fan fiction and *yaoi manga* and *anime*, while perhaps initially forms of heterosexual women's resistance, have come to represent queer cultural scenarios for a new generation of young people. What was once traded among a small group of people in the form of handmade zines is now widely available and accessible by many via the internet. And while slash and *yaoi* are lifeboats for young queer kids trying to find representations of themselves in the larger culture, they are also permeating the mainstream, creating a shift in the cultural scenarios accessed by everyone in U.S. culture. Young people—LGBTQ-identified and others—have many outlets not only for discovering queer culture but also for making their own media, media that represent their experiences, emotions, and desires, and they are able to readily share that media with others. They make up for the dearth of representations of same-sex desire and behavior in mainstream media and in sexuality education curriculum through their ability to share media via the internet.

Young people of all kinds are growing up exposed to alternatives to heteronormative cultural scripts. Sexual scripts and the sexual norms they inform are shifting with the changing culture. This cultural shift has not just opened up options for LGBTQ-identified kids; it is perhaps also queering the dominant culture, making notions of sexual and gender fluidity more acceptable. Young people growing up today are less likely to associate homosexuality with deviance and immorality and instead see it as a valid, acceptable, and progressive way to be in the world. In the chapter that follows, I show how queer notions of family are challenging the straightening process of heteropatriarchal family formations, with broad implications for all of U.S. society.

5

"It's Going to Be Okay"

Queering the Family

During the time I spent at Spectrum, Gabe was a regular attendee. He is incredibly warm and kind, with something nice to say about everyone. He enjoys playing Yu-Gi-Oh! (a *manga*-themed trading card game) and performing in the monthly drag show, where he is a beloved favorite and regularly beats out the competition in Spectrum versions of *RuPaul's Drag Race*. Gabe was one of many interviewees who, upon disclosing their sexual and/or gender identities to their parents, were surprised to be met with kindness and support. Here he describes disclosing to his father:

> There was always a general fear of what they [my mother and father] might think, what they might say, what they might do. So, I came out to a couple of my cousins first, and they were okay with it, and then I started coming to Spectrum a lot more. . . . I finally had enough courage to tell my father. I wrote him a two-page note and left it under his door for when he got back home from work, 'cause I did not know how to approach him on it at all. I kind of wrote like, about me, and I wrote that I would hope that it wouldn't change anything between us. So when he got home from work he came to me. . . . He's always put up such a tough front that I figured he would completely, like, either blow it off or deny it, kick me out over it, or I thought so many things that were the worst possible outcome. I didn't think there was going to be a positive outlook on it, so . . . when we talked about it we were kind of focusing on . . . it was more of me just telling him, "This is how I feel and this is who I am," and just, he understood it, and he listened to me when I talked and, 'cause he would ask questions about it too, . . . "How did you come to this conclusion? When did this start?" It's just, like, he would listen to me when I would answer his questions, so [he] made me feel just that much better, the fact that he

took the time to kind of talk to me, he asked questions, he listened to me, and he actually still showed that nothing was going to be any different.

While Gabe imagined many outcomes as a result of the letter he wrote his father, the idea that his father would approach him calmly and respectfully to discuss his sexuality had not crossed his mind. Although Gabe was less anxious about sharing his sexuality and gender with his mother, he still waited until he was sixteen years old and was quite nervous about her response. Not only was she supportive of him, she explained that she, too, identified as bisexual. Both of his parents were also supportive in terms of Gabe's gender non-conformance. He described how his father was protective of him, at one point taking him out of a school where he was bullied, for example. In the excerpt below, Gabe tells of his mother attending Spectrum drag shows to see him perform:

> There were several times where my mom would help me dress up for drag shows. When she manages to attend, . . . she would help people with their makeup. She'd bring a whole bunch of stuff and clothes, makeup, and she's like, "You can help yourself to whatever. If you need help with anything just let me know." She would be so supportive and she would actually be in the crowd and cheer me on when I got up, too. . . . it was kind of weird knowing that my mom was there, but it's also a great thing at the same time.

While certainly not every youth I encountered had parents who supported them in their self-discovery and identification of their sexualities and genders, I was surprised by how many did, simply because the dominant narrative about LGBTQ youth is one of family rejection. I, along with so many others, including many of the adults associated with Spectrum, took it for granted that LGBTQ-identified young people necessarily struggle with their parents and families over acceptance. But what I found in many cases was simply that they don't—at least not any more than any parent might struggle with a teenager who is becoming more sexually aware and active. In many cases, it was actually the young person, having adopted the narrative of rejection, who held back from talking to their parent. But for this particular sample of youth, their fears were not realized. Recognizing that Spectrum is a unique setting located in an urban, morally and politically liberal community, my effort to understand this phenomenon in the context of Spectrum led me to the family structures and characteristics of the youth participants. In this chapter, I suggest that the straightening effect of the Standard North American Family is weakening as all of the ways that people are queering family gain validation in U.S. culture. The shifting of norms around gender and sexuality—along with varied family formations within working-class families and families of color—have manifested themselves in the formation of family in the United States.

Resisting Family Conventions

Heteronormativity is deeply embedded in the U.S. family structure.[1] What the sociologist Dorothy E. Smith refers to as the Standard North American Family (SNAF)—a heterosexual adult pair with children, where the man is breadwinner and the woman is predominantly responsible for child care and household chores—is the first place where humans are socialized into hegemonic norms around sexuality and gender and where sexist and heterosexist oppression is first internalized.[2] This family type, while largely considered natural and normal throughout modern Western cultures, is socially and culturally contingent. As the sociologist Judith Stacey argues, "Anthropological and historical studies convince me that the family is not an institution, but an ideological, symbolic construct that has a history and a politics."[3] The symbolic triumph of the 2013 U.S. Supreme Court decisions that overturned Proposition 8 and found the Defense of Marriage Act to be unconstitutional is how they showed that the heteropatriarchal family formation that upholds norms in our culture can be successfully challenged. Recognition of same-sex marriage means that our society will have to rethink laws and norms around what formally defines a family, which could have an incredible impact on things like legal rights of parents (including what exactly defines parenthood), child custody, inheritance, and more: the very categories that have supported patriarchal, misogynist, white supremacist ideologies for so long.

Challenging the ideology of the SNAF has been an act of survival on the part of those who never had a shot at fulfilling its rigid requirements. While today we associate marriage equality with the LGBTQ movement, challenging norms around what is considered an acceptable family formation has long been the province of the working class, the poor, and people of color—of which some identify as LGBTQ, of course. Because the ideology of the SNAF is so deeply tied to privilege—white, middle-class, heterosexual privilege—any failure to fit into the proper family mold has been held as proof of individual deviance and pathology. Rather than acknowledge large structural systems of inequality that drive poverty and restrict access to critical cultural capital like education, the discourse of the failed family places the blame on female-headed households, children born out of wedlock, high rates of infidelity, and divorce.[4] Further, little is said about the value of alternative family formations, given the failure of the SNAF to actually meet people's needs, particularly those of women and children.

For example, the sociologists Michael Bennett and Juan Battle raise the argument that there is a distinct lack of inclusion of Black LGBTQ people in mainstream research and textbooks on the Black family. Using the various debates in sociological scholarship that either support or refute the now notorious Moynihan Report,[5] they argue that the debates continue to center around the notion of a heterosexual family formation. Even among the detractors of the Moynihan Report, Bennett and Battle state that research "often does not interrogate the practice of using low rates of single parenthood and divorce as measures of 'successful' families. This model fails to consider that many families, especially with LGBT parents or members, may be better off with non-married co-parents of the same sex, or the divorce of parents who are not compatible, or various extended family structures."[6] Bennett and Battle's critique is important to the argument I make here because they insist that it is a mistake to consider LGBTQ families as distinct from Black families; rather, they urge researchers to recognize how alternative family forms are the result of Black LGBTQ families. Again, the battle over family law in the United States ought not just be about same-sex marriage.

In a heteropatriarchal society, the SNAF can be an incredibly dangerous place for women and children.[7] Although the narrative of risk and threat faced by LGBTQ people tends to focus on harassment and bullying outside the home—much like the myth of the stranger rapist/pedophile as a threat to women and children—the most dangerous place for queer children is actually their home, since most physical and sexual abuse is perpetrated upon children by adults in their family.[8] Families where traditional gender roles and norms are particularly valued can create conditions for homophobic and transphobic harassment and violence.

Yet, because of its significance as a site of socialization, the family also has the most potential for inspiring radical change in society when it comes to gender and sexuality norms. The fight for marriage equality is not just about equal rights for same-sex couples in the United States; it is a very real threat to heteropatriarchy, which is arguably why the fight has met so much resistance. The sexual and gender order that has long been the undergirding structure of dominant U.S. society is threatened by the institutionalization of queer family. And while the possibility and formation of a new kind of family has been theorized and analyzed by feminist and queer scholars for decades, the Spectrum generation are really the first to have been socialized in a world where gay, lesbian, bisexual, and other non-heterosexual identified people have—on a large scale—publicly formed families.[9] Whereas their parents' generation came out in the context of a narrative that being gay meant forgoing family ties of any sort, a significant number of children of this generation are being raised by same-sex couples and queer people—whether that be their parents, their aunties and uncles, neighbors, teachers, mentors, coaches, or other important adults in their lives.[10] The possibility of a non-heterosexual existence and a reframing of the gender binary is simply more available to this generation. And even though the SNAF maintains its iron grip on normative behavior in U.S. culture, even among heterosexual, non-queer families, tolerance of same-sex sexuality and gender non-conformity has increased radically.

LGBTQ-Identified Youth and Their Parents

Even though not all parents are hostile toward their gay children, the simple absence of same-sex desire as a healthy, valid option has often foreclosed on any sense of validation a child with same-sex desires might have. Beyond simply being absent, if there is acknowledgment of homosexuality, too often it is framed as something to feel pity about, if not abhor. Of course young people internalize these spoken and unspoken messages about homosexuality and queerness that they learn from their families at a very young age, making the SNAF a key site of oppression for kids who are queer.

Despite the major shifts in LGBTQ visibility and rights witnessed by society in the past several decades, the dominant narrative about LGBTQ kids and their families continues to be one of peril. Advice for parents of LGBTQ children suggests that having a gay kid will likely be a traumatic experience, requiring one to seek professional help as it is likely to trigger grieflike emotions.[11] Having a LGBTQ-identified child is still publicly painted as a problem that needs fixing (if not a tragedy), rather than something to celebrate or even something unremarkable. Although it has historically been the case that LGBTQ-identified people have waited until they had achieved emotional and financial independence from their families before disclosing their identities, today people are disclosing LGBTQ identities at much younger ages.[12] Young people faced with disclosing details about their sexuality to their families fear rejection and abandonment, fears that too often are fueled by the barrage of claims in the news media about the precarity of LGBTQ youth.[13]

For the young people of Spectrum,[14] being out to one's parents is the rule, not the exception. A distinct lack of traumatic stories about disclosing their identities to parents, in particular for sexual-minority-identified youths, marked this group as unique in light of the dominant discourse of precarity. Compared to others, what is different about these youths that made their coming out experiences generally positive ones? What is different about their parents? Are these young people exceptions to the rule, or is there more to the taken-for-granted narrative of tragedy that surrounds LGBTQ-identified people and their families? My findings reinforce some of what we already know to be true, that gender atypical children are more likely to adopt an LGBTQ-identity at a younger age and that this is less of a shock to their already suspecting parents.[15] But they also shine light on a different trend, one that is likely the result of several decades worth of feminist and LGBTQ organizing and visibility—the queering of families. Spectrum youth typically come from non-traditional families (families that don't fit the SNAF formula) and often have an LGBTQ-identified parent and/or relative. The LGBTQ rights movement, with its focus on abolishing the closet and adopting pride for sexual and gender diversity and the resulting normalization of homosexuality, has had a profound impact on family formations in the United States.

Parents' Unexpected Reactions

While horribly destructive, acts of physical violence or abandonment are hardly the only ways that queer kids are harmed by their families. LGBTQ-identified children face the ultimate rejection by loved ones when they are simply not accepted by their families because of their gender or sexuality. Therefore many of the young people of Spectrum expressed deep anxiety and stress about the anticipation of talking to their parents about their sexual and/or gender identity.

Many of the young people I interviewed told me how scared they were to share their sexual identities with their parents. The specific fear that their parents would disown them and force them to leave the house was particularly vivid for them. After his mother discovered some gay pornography websites he had been looking at on the computer, Travon—a sixteen-year-old Black boy who identifies as queer—was terrified that he would be forced to leave the house:

> I was so embarrassed, and like, I was scared . . . I was expecting her to freak out about it 'cause, like, I've seen on movies and actually, I had seen an actual news report like, a couple days before . . . they were interviewing this entire tunnel of LGBTQ youth that were kicked out of their homes cause of who they were. It terrified me, so when she talked to me I was like, "Oh my god." So not only was I embarrassed that I was, like, looking up stuff, but I was, like, scared that I was going to be kicked out of the house at eleven [years old].

Aaron, the film buff from chapter 4, a nineteen-year-old Mexican-American man who identifies as gay, had a similar experience when his stepfather sat him down for a talk after discovering a somewhat suggestive photo of Aaron and his boyfriend:

> With my stepfather . . . I mean he asked me. I didn't come out to him, he
> asked me. And . . . I was expecting some outrage and to be kicked out of
> the house, right? What I admire the most was he held me by the hand,
> and he told me that it's going to be okay. And it's an emotional thing . . .

Aaron trailed off as he was brought to tears in recounting this story to
me, demonstrating the emotional significance of his stepfather's acceptance of him over the rejection he had expected.

Fueled by, among other things, media-driven fears about the consequences of sharing their identities with their parents, neither Travon
nor Aaron had any intention of telling their parents outright about their
sexual desires. Rather, as was often the case with Spectrum youth, their
disclosure was in some ways involuntary and a matter of circumstance.
Whether confronted by their parents, or disclosing to their parents for
the first time, in most cases, their parents were surprisingly warm and
supportive.

In fact, for some youths, coming out to their parents was a non-issue.
They were not afraid and more or less knew they would be supported.
For example, when Brian, a twenty-one-year-old white youth who
identifies as queer—he's the kid from chapter 2 who first learned what
a drag show was when he started attending Spectrum—told both his
mom and dad he was gay in seventh grade, his dad then accompanied
him on his first visit to Spectrum. He describes his experience as very
non-traumatic:

> Honestly, my coming out and my growing up gay wasn't that bad of an
> experience, I mean there were some times that were a little difficult, but
> I didn't have . . . the, you know, . . . *Lifetime* movie. . . . I wasn't kicked
> out, I wasn't abused for it. And I went to relatively good schools that were
> accepting.

Ditto, a twenty-year-old biracial youth who identifies as bisexual,
described how it felt when her dad asked her one evening on the porch
if she was gay. She says, "It was the most casual . . . it was kind of like asking me, is your favorite color blue? That's what it felt like. There was no
judging." Isaac—the fan fiction writer from chapter 4—a nineteen-year-
old multiracial Black man who identifies as gay, explains how before

she knew anything about his sexual desires, his mother had already "introduced" him to the LGBTQ community, making it clear that, in her opinion, same-sex desire was an acceptable option for him: "Another thing that influenced [my sexuality]was my mom's openness with it, so I never really had what a lot of kids have . . . this foreboding." In the case of these examples, these young people seem to have never gotten the message that being LGBTQ-identified was a problem. It was only later, when they learned that they were supposed to have been afraid, that they describe themselves as lucky or different from most kids.

Of course, not every Spectrum youth had good experiences disclosing to their parents. When I asked Miguel (a twenty-year-old Mexican man who identifies as gay) how his father reacted to him disclosing his identity, he told me his dad returned to Mexico because of it, leaving him in the United States to fend for himself (although his father has since apologized to him for reacting this way). While Adam (an eighteen-year-old white man who identifies as gay) has a very supportive mother who has always been open about the option of same-sex desire, he has had a particularly hard time getting along with his father throughout his life. The conflict with his father seems largely to do with his father's disappointment in Adam not being the son he had expected. Adam has been gender atypical his whole life, enjoying singing and dancing, dressing up in costumes and girls' clothes, and wearing nail polish. Because of his father's intolerance, Adam continues to identify to his father as bisexual rather than gay, as he feels that this identification alleviates the tension between them to some degree.

Nor was it just fathers rejecting their gay/queer sons. Lucy, a seventeen-year-old white girl who identifies as a lesbian, lives with her mother and stepfather in a rural, religiously conservative community. Lucy's mother is very punitive in her reactions to Lucy's sexual identity. Lucy's mother confronted Lucy about her sexuality after reading her diary, and in reaction to Lucy's expression of her sexual desires, she frequently takes away her posters and music and forbids her from going out of the house. Although her mother claims to not have a problem with gay people, she insists that Lucy is not a lesbian and told her once that Lucy "didn't turn out the way she thought she would."

The experiences of transgender-identified youths disclosing to their families were somewhat different compared to those disclosing sexual identities. In four out of six cases, transgender youths first told their parents they were lesbian. These four individuals were sexed female at birth, went through a period of identifying as lesbians, but not long after came to realize that what made them different from their heteronormative peers was their gender identity not their sexual identity. They therefore began to recognize themselves as transgender and not necessarily lesbian. The other two participants were sexed male at birth but never identified as gay before identifying as transgender, and both now identify their sexuality as pansexual. They were similar to the previously described group in that they initially were grappling with their sexualities, but they quickly began to realize that it was their gender identity more so than their sexual identity that was of issue. In the case of the previous four individuals, being transgender was more complicated than being lesbian, primarily because it was less understood by their parents. These individuals experienced various microaggressions from their parents, such as a parent failing to identify them with the pronouns they preferred or a parent being selective about when and where they would or would not recognize their child's gender change.

In the case of the two transwomen, both experienced extremely negative reactions from their parents to their transgender identity. They were both forbidden from dressing as girls at home and severely punished for violations. At the time I met with each of them, they were estranged from their parents and experiencing homelessness. Much like sexual identity, disclosing a transgender or genderqueer identity to family can be fraught. Norms around misogyny and sexism result in experiences being quite different for transwomen compared to transmen.

It is worth noting that in all the cases where parents reacted in a severely negative way to youth disclosure, there was evidence of lifelong dysfunction and/or abuse of the children by their parents. Consistent with Ritch Savin-Williams's argument, the youth with particularly hostile parents were coming from very unsafe family situations in which their disclosure of LGBTQ identities was just one part of the violence they were subjected to throughout their lives.[16]

Mother's Instinct

Gender atypical young people share their queer sexual identities with their parents at younger ages.[17] Those children who are particularly non-gender conforming are more likely to be confronted about their sexuality by friends and family at a younger age because of the way society conflates homosexuality with non-normative gender expression. Friends and family of flamboyant boys and butch girls often assume them to be gay or lesbian. Coinciding with this assumption, parents of gender atypical children have had some time to prepare themselves for the fact that their child might identify as lesbian, gay, or bisexual, and therefore they are less likely to react negatively and may be better equipped to deal with the disclosure when it comes. Interestingly, as mentioned above, parents and peers often push gender atypical children towards an LGB identity, sometimes only to learn later on that their child or friend is transgender-identified. The experiences I share below are those of sexual-minority-identified youths, not transgender-identified youths.

In chapter 3 I explained how certain boys described always having known they were gay and how this was often related to their gender atypicality in childhood. Particularly among the boys, when they disclosed their sexuality to their mothers, many claimed to have always known their son was gay. The youths sometimes described this experience as some version of "mother's instinct." Parents associated moments in their son's childhood where they behaved in gender atypical ways as signs of them being gay.

An eighteen-year-old white, gay man, Nik is a tall, lanky blond with blue eyes. Today his hair is buzz cut, but it used to be longer and is typically dyed a different color every time I see him. He is wearing a green and white striped tank top with a low-slung neckline, black skinny jeans rolled up into capris, a cardigan sweatshirt, and flip flops on his feet. He's got iridescent blue eye shadow on his eyelids and he kicks his crossed leg up and down gently while we talk. It was during his junior year in high school when Nik told his mother that the hickies on his neck were from a boy not a girl. When I asked him how she responded, he told me she said:

> "I always kind of knew." And I mean there was no way she couldn't've! I mean when I was four, I had watched the [musical] *Cats* VHS so many

times that I actually broke it. And she refused to replace it. I was like, "Mom!" She actually finally ended up caving in and getting another one. And then when I was in fifth grade I absolutely had to have the Cher *Ultimate Collection* CD.

Parents' conflation of sexuality with gender—in this case, Nik and his mother associating an interest in Broadway musicals with queerness—led the parents to *assume* their gender atypical child was gay, and therefore they were not surprised when this turned out to be the case. Although I'm making some assumptions here about Nik and his mother, anecdotal experience leads me to believe that had Nik been a girl obsessed with *Cats*, this would not have become a marker of a queer sexuality for either mother or daughter.

Adam, who described himself as an effeminate boy, told me that his mother always suspected he would grow up to be gay. One of the most poignant stories he shared was of a time in middle school when he was, as he describes it now, homophobic and not gay-identified. During this time he got in a dramatic fight with his mom because she suggested to him that it was okay for him to explore his feelings for boys. He reacted with anger and frustration at this suggestion:

I was like, why would you say that to me? I'm not gay! That's gross blah-blah-blah. And I had a giant episode about it. And she was in the room and she locked me out of her room and I would sit there and scream and kick at her door. And I was like, "I can't believe you're calling me gay!" And I would sit there and cry at her door because she called me gay. But she didn't even call me . . . it was, "Adam, it's okay if you're having feelings for guys," or "Adam, it's okay to explore." And I was just so appalled. I was like, "How could you even think that of me?"

Later when Adam did disclose his gay identity to his mom, she responded with, "I told you. I knew it." When Gabe, described in the introductory narrative to this chapter, talked to his mother about his sexual identity, she replied, "I've known since the day you were born." When he probed her, asking how a person could know something like that, she ascribed it to mother's intuition.

During my time at Spectrum, the agency was experiencing an unprecedented number of contacts from parents who were seeking resources for children under the age of thirteen (the minimum age for youths to attend drop-in at Spectrum). This resulted in the development of a program aimed specifically at these children and their parents that was held outside regular drop-in hours. Since they fell outside the scope of my human subjects protocol, I didn't conduct any formal research with this group. But I have anecdotal evidence, based on the few interactions I observed and my conversations with staff and interns, that the kids coming to the under-thirteen drop-in were grappling with gender identity issues more than sexual identity issues. Either the parents of these kids reached out on their own to their local LGBTQ center for help, or concerned teachers, counselors, or other community members might have referred them there. Regardless, this is an example of a significant shift in the age when parents and children begin to address matters of marginalized sexualities and genders.

One explanation for why the participants in my study so frequently disclosed their sexual identities to parents at a young age is their genderqueerness. Many of these young people expressed queer genders, therefore their parents, conflating sexuality and gender, suspected they might eventually identify as gay. Similarly, the lack of negative experiences might also be due to the fact that the parents of these children had more time than other parents to prepare themselves for that moment when their child might disclose to them and therefore were able to react in a mild manner. But not all of the youths of Spectrum could be described as genderqueer. What follows is a discussion about the queering of family and its effect on youths' experiences disclosing their identities to their families.

Queering Family

Exposure to LGBTQ-identified parents, relatives, and family friends was another common characteristic among the young people of Spectrum. Eight of the mothers or fathers of youths interviewed claimed a gay, bisexual, lesbian, or pansexual identity, meaning that more than 20 percent of the people I interviewed had an LGBTQ parent. Similarly, of the youths I interviewed, nine had gay, lesbian, or bisexual brothers and sisters. In fact, there are two pairs of siblings among my participants. Youths in my interview pool identified fourteen LGBTQ cousins, aunts, uncles, godparents, and grandmothers in their families (not to mention several other friends of the family). These youths constituted more than two-thirds of the youths I interviewed.

This demonstrates that a significant number of the youths who are LGBTQ and attending Spectrum on a regular basis have been exposed to LGBTQ people in their family circles. In liberal, urban communities like the one where Spectrum is located, the normalization and routinization of same-sex desire, behavior, and relationships has resulted in far less stigma being attached to homosexuality today than in decades past.[18] Many more people identify—in friend, family, and professional circles—as LGBTQ, therefore it is not surprising that so many of the young people of Spectrum have adult LGBTQ family members, particularly aunts, uncles, and cousins. But it is also likely that being LGBTQ at a younger age is aided by the reality of having an LGBTQ-identified parent or sibling, simply because early exposure to same-sex desire, same-sex relationships, and gender atypicality presents this identity as a viable option for these youths. In other words, LGBTQ-identified family members, particularly parents, are counterhegemonic to compulsory heterosexuality.

Trevor, a twenty-year-old white man, first identified as bisexual, then as gay, not long after he got out of high school. A daily regular at Spectrum since I started coming, he is a bit naïve for his age. He's a round-faced kid with acne, a gap between his two front teeth, and a warm, joyful smile. He often wears oversized, black pants that are covered in buckles, pockets, and zippers, along with concert T-shirts of his favorite bands. He's often sporting various accessories purchased from Hot Topic, like a pink faux fur hat that hangs down like ponytails on either side of his face and fingerless gloves. Although he is a fan of all kinds of music, he is crazy about Lady Gaga and names her first when I ask him to tell me who the most important people in his life are. Trevor has been raised by his grandparents. He told me it was through his introduction to his estranged lesbian sister that he learned about being LGBTQ:

That's how it kind of all started and then I started getting involved with my sister and her partner. . . . And then, um, so then, that was like, the really big start of me getting to know more about the LGBTQ people and stuff like that. And then, um, I remember that I first came out as bisexual.

This is not to suggest that LGBTQ-identified parents necessarily raise LGBTQ-identified children, as research shows that correlations between sexual identity of parents and the sexual identity of their children should not be confused with causation. Rather, as the sociologists Judith Stacey and Timothy J. Biblarz argue, the influence a parents' sexuality—heterosexuality included—has on the sexuality of their child has more to do with patterns of gender roles and cultural socialization than it does with any notion of inherent sexual orientation.[19] Young people who are presented with alternatives to compulsory heterosexuality may be more open to exploring their feelings of same-sex desire as well as more open to assigning an identity label to those feelings such as lesbian, gay, or bisexual. Similarly, youths who spend time with transgender or gender atypical family and friends may be more open to questioning and exploring their gender identity.

It's also worth noting that lack of exposure to LGBTQ identities results in a different framing of queer sexualities and genders. In his discussion of space and sexuality, Jack Halberstam reflects on the experiences of "rural queers," suggesting how little they may have in common with LGBTQ-identified people in U.S. urban areas: "In climates where homosexual identity is not forbidden but simply unthinkable, the pre-adult sexual subject who pursues same-sex eroticism may do so without necessarily assuming that this sexual activity speaks the truth of one's identity."[20] I use Halberstam here to show how sexual identity formation is influenced by space and place, suggesting that "normal" is contingent on the context within which you live.

Ernie learned from and felt supported by his mother's roommate, who at the time we spoke was a transwoman, but who was living as a man when they first met. He told his mother's roommate he was gay before telling his mom:

Me and her would talk all the time. Well, before, she was a drag queen. So she would do drag. And sometimes . . . she would sneak me in the club with her when she'd do her drag shows. So that was cool, but me and her would just talk. . . . At first I was like, "What are you talking about?"

Both Trevor and Ernie describe how LGBTQ family members and family friends had a profound impact on their understanding of themselves as LGBTQ-identified. Consistent with stories told by other participants, these LGBTQ family members often encouraged the youths to embrace their identities and provided the support they needed to do so.

In and of itself, this finding is not a surprising one. But it's important to reflect on how the queering of family has implications for the larger U.S. society. The visibility of LGBTQ people in U.S. society has meant not only that most people know someone who is LGBTQ but that most people are likely to have a family member or loved one who identifies as LGBTQ, therefore compassion through empathy for a friend or family member has been a powerful strategy of the LGBTQ rights movement. It has also meant that even within traditional SNAF structures, tolerance, if not acceptance, of LGBTQ people has been on the rise. This broadening tolerance and acceptance results in expanded options for everyone. This process of normalization has resulted in a paradigm shift when it comes to U.S. culture and homosexuality. The youth of Spectrum—and their adolescent peers—have grown up in the midst of this normalization that their parents' generation has worked to achieve. This has resulted in more LGBTQ-identified young people, but, more important, it has also resulted in a shift in how all young people form their sexual subjectivities.

Non-Traditional Family

As mentioned above, growing up genderqueer and having LGBTQ-identified parents and other adults in their lives both might explain why some of the Spectrum youth had non-traumatic experiences sharing their sexualities and genders with their parents at relatively young ages. Another important reason that parents of these youth were more accepting of them may be that their family formations don't resemble the SNAF model. In particular, a lack of conformity to traditional gender roles, adherence to secular rather than religious belief systems, and life-course patterns that differ from the middle-class norm were characteristics of the families of many of the Spectrum youths I spoke with.

Among the family characteristics of the study's participants, it was striking how few of them came from households that fit the SNAF model with a father and a mother who fulfilled traditional gender roles. I saw this manifested in several different ways, including father-headed single-parent households (five), mother-headed single-parent households (eleven), and LGBTQ-identified parents (two lesbian mothers, three bisexual mothers, three gay fathers, and one pansexual father). For example, this is how Isaac describes his mom, who has raised him without his father's involvement:

> My mom is . . . to put it like very bluntly, sort of the hippie mom. She struggled a bit with me growing up being that I was like a first child, and when my father left, she had to play the role of both the disciplinarian and the nurturer. So it got a bit confusing for a while. But she's always been really open and accepting of basically everything.

Even among the youths who grew up in a household with a heterosexual parent couple, there were often things that suggested that the parents were not modeling traditional gender roles. These include both parents typically working outside of the home and family structures where the mother was more often the biological parent of the child and therefore the dominant parent in the family.[21] These parents were often described by their children as rebellious, as having been teen parents, and/or as having had children from multiple partners. One mother had a burgeoning career as a professional dominatrix. The youths of Spectrum had fathers who were primary nurturers and mothers who were wage earners. I would characterize few of their parents as fulfilling traditional gender roles.

Devout religiosity can often be a driver for the maintenance of traditional gender roles in the family.[22] While the majority of people interviewed did associate their upbringing with some nod to religion (only nine youths did *not* identify their families as being religious at all), only a small handful were raised in a devoutly religious home. Two youths who were siblings were raised practicing Wicca, a religion that rejects the traditional family and gendered ideologies of the Judeo-Christian majority in the United States. Another youth became an evangelical Christian of his own accord in late adolescence but was raised by nonreligious parents. The fourth was raised by a devoutly Catholic mother and identifies himself as a devout Catholic. Among the other youths who identified themselves with a religion, they typically described their families as being casually religious, attending church irregularly, if at all. Or, as was often the case, they may have had devoutly religious grand-parents who exposed the youths to religion, but their parents had not maintained a strict religious practice in the home. When I asked Gabe if his family practiced religion, he explained that his maternal grand-mother was religious and would sometimes "ride" him and his cousins about religion, but his parents were not:

> My grandmother, she's, the term I would use is "overly Christian." So . . . she's kind of targeted me, she's targeted my cousins . . . she still accepts us and everything, but she has her moments where she just kind of, like, rides on us just a little bit. She apologizes for it every time but just, there are times where . . . she's the only one who's really had any negative out-look on it in any way when it comes down to religion. . . . One thing that I enjoy about my family is that we're all kind of, like really open with reli-gion. . . . We believe different aspects of all kinds of different religions so in a way we all kind of live in our own kind of religion that best suits us. So there was like never any religious pressure or anything.

More important, while many of the youths had stories about attending worship, being involved with a church at one point, and in some cases experiencing discrimination in these spaces, I would not describe their home lives as devoutly religious. With the exception of two white, gay men who had Catholic family members, religion was not mentioned by participants as a point of contention when it came to disclosing their identities to their parents. It is clear that secular belief systems are more prominent among these young people and their families and could be a contributing factor to parental tolerance and acceptance of an LGBTQ-identified child.

Finally, the SNAF model relies on conforming to a dominant series of normative middle-class life-course stages that include getting a col-lege education and pursuing a career, marriage with a suitable partner, and having children, strictly in that order.[23] This life-course pattern may simply not be an option for many people living in poverty, for members of the working class, and for some communities of color that bear the legacy of centuries of economic disadvantage and oppression. Considering that graduating high school was a challenge for many of them, the opportunity to attend college and earn a degree seems out of reach for many of the youth of Spectrum. Many people outside of the middle and upper classes in the United States do not get an education, start a career, get married, and have children, in that order. Their lives follow a different course, sometimes one that does not include college and a career at all and, in many cases, one in which children come before or outside of a marriage.

Are parents who hold more dearly to middle-class expectations of life-course patterns more deeply disappointed when they learn their child is not going to conform to a heteronormative pathway? Perhaps the parents of Spectrum youth did not see their child's gender or sexual nonconformity as a sign of failure, either theirs or their child's. Further, the middle-class pressure on parents who see their children as extensions of their own success doesn't extend in the same way to the families described here.[24] This does not mean that these parents do not hold high hopes for their children; rather, what those hopes are and how they manifest themselves as successes and failures are different for families outside of the hegemonic norm. The very fact that many of the youths' parents had themselves not followed the dominant path towards a SNAF family formation may be a reason for their compassion for their queer kids.

The Counter Hegemonic Power of Queer Families

Most of the participants in this study had relatively positive experiences with their parents regarding the disclosure of their sexual identities, and they identified as LGBTQ to their parents at a rather early stage in their lives. These positive experiences might be due to the gender non-normative behavior of the child, which prepares parents in advance for the possibility of having a child who identifies as LGBTQ. Further, I suggest that having LGBTQ-identified family members and the nontraditional nature of the child's family structure may be significant factors in how families respond to their LGBTQ-identified kids. While it should come as no surprise to the reader that the more traditional (and hegemonically normal) the family formation, the less tolerance there is for queerness in its midst, this discussion serves to remind all of us that the battle over family and marriage is not just one that belongs to the LGBTQ movement. The far-reaching implications of marriage equality—as an LGBTQ initiative—has the power to reorganize one of the most entrenched social norms in our society.

As the sociologist Jessica Fields shows in her study on Parents and Friends of Lesbians and Gays (PFLAG) members, parents' anxieties about having sexual minority-identified or gender atypical children are linked to the parents' heteronormative expectations of their children: that they will grow up to marry and have children and that they will not be queer in a society that rewards normality.[25] Yet the queering of family, as demonstrated by the experiences of Spectrum youth, likely contributes to parents' positive reception to the disclosure of their LGBTQ-identified children because the less invested parents are in being normal, the less of a threat a queer child poses to their sense of themselves as "good" parents.

Further, queer family formations are counterhegemonic to compulsory heterosexuality and the SNAF. The gender order has shifted profoundly in the last fifty years, and parental acceptance of LGBTQ-identified children, along with young people's understanding of gender as malleable and unstable, could very well be part of the result. In the book *Gaga Feminism*, Jack Halberstam discusses the possibilities that open up in the face of queer family:

> The butch dad and the femme mom raise the possibility of authority without patriarchy (because the butch does not access male privilege), gender polarity without compulsory heterosexuality (because the femme does not always access heterosexual privilege), and they make possible an education for potentially gender-normative kids in the arbitrariness of all gender roles—so kids raised by a femme mother and a butch father might learn about gendered forms of power untethered to gender hierarchies; they might see masculinity and femininity as more malleable, and they might understand gender as something that someone does rather than something someone is.[26]

Children raised within family formations that reject the dominant gender order—or what has historically been the dominant gender order—are not likely to reproduce that order themselves. These changes have implications across all family formations, including those that are formed around heterosexuality.

The stories shared here by the youths of Spectrum contradict the discourse of tragedy, danger, and risk that surrounds the phenomenon of LGBTQ children coming out to their parents. Of course, for some parents, learning that their child is LGBTQ-identified is upsetting or perhaps even tragic, and for some young people, telling their parents about their sexuality is risky, if not outright dangerous. But, with changing cultural acceptance of sexual diversity and gender atypicality, perhaps more parents will learn to celebrate their children's sexual and gender development—queer or otherwise—as a regular process of self-discovery, maturity, and independence, a complement to their roles as parents in their children's lives, and not as a sign of their failure.

A non-traditional family structure opens the options available to a young person, particularly at an exploratory stage of their lives. Homosexuality is a modern social construction, the definition of which is dependent upon biological and psychological presumptions about sexuality. At the same time, we have entered a postmodern era in which we understand sexuality and gender to be socially and historically constructed, not simply biological. We have shifted from defining homosexuality as pathology to the adoption of identities that more accurately reflect the fluidity of individual sexual and gendered desires, behaviors, and communities. Exposure—through family and peers, media, and other cultural resources—to same-sex desire, sexual fluidity, and the expansion of categories and options for identification results in a larger group of young people who are more willing to explore their same-sex desires in a visible way. In other words, queer sexualities are the result of the destabilization of fixed categories. Youth sexualities reflect this instability as adolescents begin the journey of discovering and exploring their sexual selves. The young people of Spectrum and their peers across the country are learning how to be sexual and gendered beings in an era in which LGBTQ rights are more and more being accepted as human rights. They are the children of a generation that invested in dismantling patriarchal systems of oppression. Therefore their explorations of self reflect a more open, fluid, queer relationship to sexuality and gender.

Because heteropatriarchy is the bedrock of the SNAF, this adoption of fluidity as a way to understand sexuality and gender has profound implications for family formation now and into the future. Heteropatriarchal family structures limit young people's sexual options. They are the normal that queer is organized in opposition to. What does a society that rejects heteronormativity look like? Have we achieved the goal of eliminating the closet? Are we moving toward a society in which LGBTQ identities are not just celebrated but perhaps unremarkable? Or will it simply be the case that same-sex attractions, couplings, and family formations will be acceptable only insomuch as they resemble the heteronormative? I reflect on these questions and more in the conclusion.

Conclusion

The New Normal Isn't Queer

It's not . . . sketched out for me who I am. I don't got a guide-book. . . . Who I am is just who I am, and I'm always trying to question that and put it into words. I'm trying to define the indefinable: me. And like, it just, it doesn't work. There's a lot of inner, internal conflict with this. . . . I always want to put myself in a box. Society puts you in enough boxes and then I'm sitting here trying to put myself in another one, like, I'm trying to figure out every aspect of who I am as if I'm thinking about myself as if I'm a different person; as if I'm trying to judge or characterize a different person.
—Travon, sixteen-year old, identifies as Black, queer, male

We are facing a sea change in norms around sexuality and gender in U.S. culture. Homosexuality, as a form of sexual conduct, increasingly fails to automatically signify one's sexual identity or orientation. Mainstream acknowledgment of transgender people is becoming commonplace. There has been a rapid proliferation of sexual and gender identities people may adopt to communicate their desires, orientations, and sense of self to others. Notions of binary sex, gender, and sexuality are giving way to fluidity and pluralism. Given this paradigm shift, we are likely to see a loosening around the categories that make up what we now consider the LGBTQ community as sexual and gender variety and fluidity become more integrated into society.

LGBTQ politics—and, by default, all LGBTQ-identified people— occupy the middle ground of a battle between normal and queer. On the one hand, the LGBTQ movement strives toward social equality for LGBTQ-identified people, while, on the other, the queer critique argues that the very identities that the movement has based its political goals upon are unstable. I have shown how adolescent negotiation of sexuality and gender is rife with ambiguity, confusion, and uncertainty. LGBTQ-identified youth in particular make visible the processes of *becoming* while simultaneously demystifying the process of naturalization. Teenagers struggle with understanding who they are, not because their essence has yet to materialize, but rather because they have yet to learn the rules of the game. As adults we forget the various processes by which we were socialized to be sexual and gendered beings. But Travon demonstrates in his statement above that young people are not born in a box that will neatly describe them forever; rather, as they grow up, they seek out existing boxes that align with who they feel they are.

Where the negotiation of gender and sexuality is the most visible is in the gray area between binary categories. Youths' explorations of non-binary sexualities and transgender identities indicate not only a conscious resistance to adopting a binary category but empirical evidence that the recognized identity categories (straight, gay, lesbian, man, woman) fail to encompass the lived experiences of individuals. Sexual desires may be innate to human experience, but our understanding of them as same-sex or other-sex in their orientation is a sociohistorical artifact. The fact that our taken-for-granted assumptions about biological sex—that one is either a boy or girl—are inaccurate renders any natural correlations among biological sex, gender, and sexuality false.[1]

The New Queer

Throughout *Growing Up Queer* I have shown how the queer-oriented youth of Spectrum struggle with being othered by a society that depends on normalization as a form of disciplinary power while at the same time finding promise in deviating from straight culture. By paying attention to intersecting forms of penalty and privilege, the experiences of Spectrum youth demonstrate that queerness is not simply a matter of one's sexuality or gender but is tied to race, class, ability, and other identity categories, making it a mistake to generalize about an LGBTQ subject.[2] It's important that we pay attention to the forces of normalization that sort out members of society, particularly in the context of a white supremacist *and* capitalist economic and political structure. If normal relies on queer to prop itself up, as LGBTQ becomes the new normal, what becomes the new queer? This is why I stress a distinction between the mainstream LGBTQ community and queer-oriented others like the youth of Spectrum.

In his memoir about having a gay son, *Oddly Normal: One Family's Struggle to Help Their Teenage Son Come to Terms with His Sexuality*, *New York Times* correspondent John Schwartz talks at length about how he and his wife, Jeanne, suspected their son was gay from a very early age. Schwartz explains that, among their peers in a highly educated, well-to-do, liberal enclave in the northeastern United States, one was not disappointed about having a gay child. Schwartz understands sexuality—whether straight or gay—to be natural and biological and "as baked into who you are as eye color and height."[3] While the Schwartz's story about their son Joseph is compelling and heartfelt, in many ways it is less a story about having a gay child and more about a parent's desperate search for an explanation as to why his child is so odd. From early childhood, Joseph struggled with succeeding at school, was diagnosed with a variety of learning disabilities, attended therapy, and acted up in various ways. Schwartz describes how Joseph's trouble at school ramped up in second grade: "As the year progressed, the teacher seemed to get overwhelmed with the daily grind of school, and she had less energy to deal with Joseph's problems and moods. His anger was close to the surface, and meltdowns were growing more common. Some students made a game of making him blow up, like the boy who would enrage Joseph by calling him 'Lemonhead' every time he wore his yellow raincoat. . . . Other kids would hide his sweatshirt at recess, day after day, to see him fall apart when he couldn't find it. Each outburst humiliated him more."[4] Joseph begins to disclose his feelings of same-sex desire first to his parents but later at school, which results in a humiliating experience and a failed suicide attempt.

Throughout the book Schwartz associates Joseph's queerness with his latent homosexuality. The story becomes one of hopefulness and survival as Joseph starts to regularly attend a community-based drop-in center for LGBTQ youth and begins to form a gay identity. In my interpretation, it was not the case that the Schwartzes were unhappy about having a gay child. Rather, their struggle was with having a child with a learning disability, who was bullied and disciplined frequently at school, and who was not popular among his peers.

Coincidentally, the same year that *Oddly Normal* was published, Jack Halberstam published *Gaga Feminism: Sex, Gender, and the End of Normal*, which I have quoted from earlier. Halberstam, an English professor and director of the Center for Feminist Research at the University of Southern California, describes his own gender as "improvised at best, uncertain and mispronounced more often than not, irresolvable and ever shifting."[5] While Schwartz's memoir is about his family's struggle with having a queer child, Halberstam's book is a call to arms for a new kind of feminism that rejects the category of normal entirely. "Gaga feminism" is described as "a gender politics that recognizes the ways in which our ideas of the normal or the acceptable depend completely upon racial and class-based assumptions about the right and the true."[6] Halberstam is decidedly not interested in creating a place where being gay or lesbian is normal, instead having aspirations that a new generation of young people will grow up with radical ideas about sex, gender, and sexuality, resisting the heteronormative impulse to adopt gay, straight, or lesbian and male or female identities, and as a result, upend the racist and classist harms caused by normalization.

These two artifacts of early twenty-first century culture exemplify the tensions that were reverberating throughout Spectrum, The Resource, the larger LGBTQ community, and U.S. society itself while I conducted this research. On the one hand, being gay or lesbian is more normalized than perhaps ever before, best demonstrated by the recent hard-fought success of the right-to-marriage movement. On the other hand, many LGBTQ-identified people are leading a revolution in terms of shifting society's understanding of sex, gender, and sexuality in the direction of the queer. The more we learn about sexuality and gender, the less salient identity categories like gay, lesbian, and straight or man and woman become.

For Halberstam, the significance of a Gaga feminism is in its potential to remake society. This vision rings true with the experiences of the young people of Spectrum. The way their experiences as queer adolescents differ from generations that came before them is evidence of a shift in society. Halberstam states, "We do not think about how changes in one sphere create changes in other spheres: and so the momentous shifts in the meaning of gender and sex and sexuality that have allowed for the emergence of transgenders and transsexuals globally have also created massive, if unnoticed, shifts in the meaning of heterosexuality, male and female."[7] These shifts will also have significant effects on the heteropatriarchal laws that govern social behavior as well, as I argued earlier. As meanings attached to sexuality, sex, and gender shift, so will the identity categories that the LGBTQ rights movement has depended upon to maintain its momentum. Can the movement withstand a fundamental shift in the way society thinks about and understands gender and sexuality? Is this a shift away from identity politics?

Yet where does that leave Joseph Schwartz and the "oddly normal" youth of Spectrum who daily are facing *institutional* sources of oppression whose distinct purpose is to normalize? The pressure is unrelenting upon these young people to figure out who they are as they merge into adulthood. Although Travon resists putting himself into a box, this moment of time as an adolescent may be the only period in his life that he will have the luxury to claim to not know who he is. The institutions that govern society do not allow for ambiguity with respect to identity— whether referring to sexuality, gender, or, as I discuss below, even citizenship status.[8] But for society to advocate for the most marginalized among us, it is profoundly important to acknowledge the way that sexualities, genders, and other identity categories are formed, transformed, validated, and contested.

Not Just Sexuality and Gender

In June 2012, right in the thick of my time at Spectrum, the youth movement to slow the Obama administration's rate of deportation of undocumented immigrants and to raise awareness about the plight of Dreamers—young, undocumented immigrants whose parents brought them to the United States as minors—reached its pinnacle. As part of the Campaign for the American DREAM (CAD), a group of Dreamers set out in May to walk from California to Washington, DC, to raise awareness about the DREAM Act and immigration reform. In Spectrum's hometown, young people staged a days-long consciousness-raising event about the issue.

At Spectrum, Miguel (a twenty-year-old gay man) is an undocumented Mexican migrant who as a minor was brought to the United States by his father and was particularly interested in the immigrant rights actions taking place. I arrived at Spectrum one afternoon to find Miguel and Aaron painting a big banner for the protest. Painted in black on a long, white sheet of butcher paper, it said "Stop the Deportations!" Miguel and Aaron had been going to the site of the protest to show their support for the movement, but Miguel explained that it was hard to find the location. He thought his sign could be held out on a busy street nearby, where it would attract more attention to what was happening. He explained to me that the previous evening there had been a candlelight vigil where he had spontaneously joined others in speaking publicly as an undocumented youth. He told me how scared he had been and how his voice quavered as he "came out" as undocumented to the crowd. Even though he was afraid, in the face of all of the young people risking their safety in the name of immigrant rights for all, he felt he had to speak up. That summer, as the CAD walk made its way through town, there were many parallels drawn between the Dreamer activists and the LGBTQ movement's strategies; both are formerly hidden populations taking a risk by coming out and claiming pride in their identities in the face of potentially severe consequences.

A few days later, Miguel and Aaron showed up to Spectrum in the afternoon. Aaron had just picked Miguel up from his job at a restaurant where he washes dishes. Miguel, normally cheerful and energetic, looked exhausted and said it was really hot in the kitchen at work. It's remarkable to me how down he looks when he comes from work compared to his usual self. He hates his job and would really like to attend college, but because of his immigration status he would have to pay out-of-state tuition to do so. Since we had last seen each other, the Obama administration had announced an executive order to address some of the barriers Dreamers faced. This was not a passage of the DREAM Act, but it was a temporary remedy, the Deferred Action for Childhood Arrivals (DACA).[9] I asked Miguel if he was happy about the news. He stated he was but that, at the same time, he'd lately had to take a break from Facebook and the news on the matter in general, as it was wearing on him emotionally. In the end, Miguel never applied for DACA status. He felt it wasn't enough and that he would keep agitating for more just reform.

I use this account of Miguel's experience as an example of a queer orientation that moves beyond sexuality and/or gender. Historically, undocumented youth in the United States have lived hidden lives where they appear to be just like all of their peers until they graduate from high school and no longer have access to the same paths forward. Some undocumented youths have known about their status for much of their lives, while for others it comes as a surprise as they begin to approach various markers of adulthood like applying for college or getting driver's licenses and identification cards. Undocumented young people become marginalized in society as they become adults. Vulnerable to labor exploitation and economic uncertainty, unable to access health insurance, unable to travel far, they experience depression and mental health challenges as they lose connections with peers who set off on a path toward adulthood with fewer barriers. Undocumented youth end up on paths that stray from the straight lines that govern so many other people's life course. Being gay, as I learned from interviewing and spending time with Miguel, is a very important part of who he is, but in terms of his day-to-day struggles, being undocumented is a much bigger barrier to his quality of life. The point is that Miguel is both gay and undocumented, he is not one without the other, so how do we as a society make room for the multiple ways that youth experience marginalization?

The hegemonic power of heteropatriarchy and its racialized, gendered, classed implications are deeply significant to the formation of identity for the young people in my study. Almost three decades ago, Gayle Rubin predicted that some forms of homosexuality would become acceptable within the "charmed circle" of sexuality. But she also predicted that many sexualities would remain banished to the "outer limits."[10] Rubin likened the growing acceptance of some sexualities, along with the continued exclusion of others, to racism.[11] But as many have argued, race—and other embodiments and identities—are intrinsic to the boundaries that form the charmed circle in the first place.[12] Heteropatriarchy isn't *like* racism, it *is* racist.

Therefore it will behoove us to be careful that efforts to support queer young people are not limited to just sexuality and gender. Marginalization occurs not just to LGBTQ kids but also to children with disabilities, children of color—Black and Latinx kids in particular—immigrants, children in poverty, and those who are not Catholic or Protestant Christian, to name a few. Of course, the more marginalization one embodies simultaneously, the more vulnerable to interpersonal and state violence one is likely to be. Must opportunities for validation and support of youth push them into over-identifying with their sexuality or gender compared to their other identities? Similarly, how might the over-emphasis on sexual and gender identities result in masking other sources of marginalization?

Moving beyond Identities

By describing the youth of Spectrum as queer oriented, I have attempted to show how some bodies—both consciously and unconsciously—resist the straightening effects of heteronormativity. I have argued here that not all LGBTQ-identified people are queer, and I have suggested that queerness is about characteristics beyond sexuality and gender. Without negating how some youths self-identify as queer, the use of a queer orientation allows me to move beyond a strictly identity-based conversation about sexual and gender minorities and toward one focused on structural drivers of inequality. I think it's a way out of the rut that identity politics gets stuck in. Rights-based policies that protect LGBTQ-identified people rely on the ability to be able to accurately identify who is and is not LGBTQ. Yet as we have learned from the youth of Spectrum, this is an elusive subject to nail down. As human rights regimes expand to a global level, the ability to define a category that is socially, culturally, geographically, and historically situated becomes harder and harder to do. If human rights protections insist on protecting LGBTQ people, as opposed to protecting those who resist normalization, then only those people who can successfully pass as LGBTQ will be protected.[13] Given that this very individualistic approach to rights is a product of a largely U.S.-centric worldview, the result is an imposition of individualism onto societies that are more collective and cooperative in character.[14] It also results in the reification of identity, whereby arguments made *against* LGBTQ rights are made in the name of rights of straight people. The North Carolina bathroom legislation, for example, uses arguments for the rights of women and children as its defense.

Organizing or providing services under the banner "LGBTQ youth" is limiting both because it requires participants to locate themselves within the context of sexual and gender identities and because it misses the opportunity to amass a broader spectrum of youths who are queer for reasons other than their sexuality or gender. No matter how much access the mainstream LGBTQ rights movement accomplishes with its current liberal strategies, the youth of Spectrum will likely continue to exist outside of its boundaries because of the ways in which they are excluded from and resist the hegemonic sexual order.

It is not my intention to devalue the successful efforts of identity-based rights movements that rocked the second half of the twentieth century. Rather, what I learned from the youth of Spectrum points to a particular way forward, where the spirit of democracy goes beyond formal legal recognitions to include an ethical spirit of honoring and respecting difference.[15] It is no longer enough for progressive politics in U.S. society to honor the rights of so-called LGBTQ people on the basis of people having been "born that way"; rather, difference should be honored because it is the right thing to do. What's exciting about queer orientation is that it manifests a cross-coalitional politics that some have argued went missing with the neoliberal political turn U.S. politics took in the wake of the Civil Rights Act.[16] Given that the most powerful criticisms of identity movements and their various movements for social justice are that they are essentializing, queerness as an identity, a theory, and a political movement includes multiple axes of oppression, from anti-racism organizing, to the rise in disability studies, to fat positivity movements, and therefore is inherently coalitional.

Let me be clear that I am neither arguing for a queer-er world nor a world without queerness (where all difference is accepted as "normal"). Rather, what would it mean to honor that which deviates from the normal because it is necessary to our humanity? Sara Ahmed explains it this way:

> Queer is not available as a line that we can follow, and if we took such a line, we would perform a certain injustice to those queers whose lives are lived for different points. For me, the important task is not so much finding a queer line but asking what our orientation toward queer moments of deviation will be. If the object slips away, if its face becomes inverted, if it looks odd, strange, out of place, what will we do? If we feel oblique, where will we find support?[17]

The queer movement has been powerful in that it has not been solely concerned with the rights of gender and sexual minorities; rather, it has engaged in the critique of capitalist, neoliberal politics that results in the marginalization of all queer people. Given the particular challenges that progressive politics face under the current conservative administration, the time is ripe for social justice movements that lead us toward organizing in a way that is less about the liberal political goals of accessing equal rights for various identity groups and more about coming together across difference toward similar goals of democracy, by focusing our efforts on the most marginalized among us.

Coalitional Social Justice Organizing

Two twenty-first-century social movements that exemplify the kind of multicoalitional, queer organizing that I mention above are Black Lives Matter (BLM) and the transgender movement.

Black Lives Matter, which began spontaneously as a hashtag and has grown into one of the most high-profile, international grassroots movements of our time, was founded in 2013 by Black, queer women—Alicia Garza, Patrisse Cullors, and Opal Tometi—in reaction to the murder of an adolescent Black boy, Trayvon Martin, and the resulting acquittal of his killer, George Zimmerman. Although the name "Black Lives Matter" may appear on the surface to simply be a movement about the liberation of Black people, the mission of what is now a global network of member-led chapters is deeply intersectional, addressing gender, sexuality, ability, class, nationality, and more. As the "Herstory" page on the organization's website explains, "Black liberation movements in this country have created room, space, and leadership mostly for Black heterosexual, cisgender men—leaving women, queer and transgender people, and others either out of the movement or in the background to move the work forward with little or no recognition. As a network, we have always recognized the need to center the leadership of women and queer and trans people."[18] One of the beliefs that guides the work of Black Lives Matter is that the liberation of all of us is bound up in the liberation of those most marginalized among us: "We work vigorously for freedom and justice for Black people and, by extension, all people."[19]

Similarly, the transgender movement, a broad collection of grassroots efforts towards trans* recognition and inclusion, is also inherently intersectional. Recognizing that the most at-risk trans* people are transwomen who are poor and working-class people of color, the movement is simply not just about transphobia but about racism, classism, and sexism, as well. Using the difficulty transgender people face accessing accurate identity documents as an example, in her book *Transgender History* Susan Stryker explains that "the restrictions on movement in the post-9/11 United States give transgender people more in common with immigrants, refugees, and undocumented workers than they might have with the gay and lesbian community."[20] Both Stryker and Dean Spade—among others—have shown how the administration of gender by the bureaucratic state has resulted in a transgender justice movement that "increasingly involves joining campaigns and struggles that might seem at first to have little to do with gender identity or expression—but everything to do with how the state polices those who differ from social norms and tries to solve the bureaucratic problems that arise from attempting to administer the lives of atypical members of its population."[21] Therefore efforts at addressing discrimination and hate crimes targeting trans* people are intersectional.

Without recognizing and making visible the white heteropatriarchal privilege that bolsters the mainstream LGBTQ rights movement, we run the risk of continuing to reproduce the same, tired bigotry that continues to poison the well of social justice efforts in the United States.

Spectrum and the Promise of Queer

What makes Spectrum so important to the lives of the youth who spend time there is that it validates their humanity. At Spectrum, young people who have spent their lives feeling out of place, unrecognizable, and queer meet others who have lived their lives feeling the same way. Beyond simply finding peers who share their experiences, the youth of Spectrum are validated by adults, too. Adult staff and volunteers not only recognize and affirm queerness but encourage it by, among other things, teaching the proud history of the LGBT and queer movements, passing on the revered drag tradition, and hosting queer prom as a valid alternative to the heteronormative initiation of the high school prom. For queer young people, Spectrum is an oasis of inclusion in a desert of exclusion.

Early in my field research, I participated in a sex education workshop at Spectrum. There were about six youth present along with César and myself. The focus for the module was on sexuality and gender. César began the session by explaining terms we use to describe sex and gender. Sexual orientation is similar to being left- or right-handed. Sexual identity is how you come out to folks. Sexual behavior is "who you do" and can occur along a spectrum with heterosexuality on one end and homosexuality on the other and lots of iterations in between. For gender, he explained that one has a biological sex, which is your genitals, hormones, and chromosomes; a gender identity, again, similar to being left- or right-handed; and a gender expression, which is the gender you appear to be to others, along a spectrum of femininity and masculinity. The point of these definitions is to make it clear to the group that sexuality and gender do not always line up the way folks think they should and particularly not how the heterosexual world wants them to. One participant appreciated this information, stating that sometimes he wakes up feeling manly and sometimes he wakes up feeling "femmy." Another was vexed by the fact that being bisexual meant people were always telling him he had to choose.

One of the activities involved examining stereotypes about LGB and T people's sexual behavior. Some examples of sexualized stereotypes the group came up with included things like "lesbian bed death," gay men using drugs and hooking up randomly with other men, and that trans* people are either assumed to be sex workers or asexual.[22] The exercise allowed us to speak honestly about these negative stereotypes, then think about how we are sometimes guilty of reproducing them in our own lives. César asked the group to look at how stereotypes get attached to gender norms. For example, he stated that, among gay men, "straight acting" is really code for "masculine." He pushed the group to consider how sometimes LGBTQ-identified people reproduce normative gender roles in their sexual and intimate relationships. He then countered this notion by pointing out how LGBTQ-identified people, in many cases, have more gender egalitarian relationships than straight-identified people and how straight people are learning from their queer peers how to do relationships better. César explained that there are so few gay role models for queer folks to relate to, and we questioned whether that was good or bad. I stated that there are too many bad role models for straight people, while one of the youths pointed out that queer people get to write the book, in a sense, because there are no rules. César echoed this comment, that being queer is already deviant, so crossing the line into deviant sexual behavior may be less scary for queer folks. Someone else suggested that queer people are better at experimenting and then deciding if they do or don't like something. I love the way this conversation shows the promise of queerness and queer youth in particular. It demonstrates that sexualized stereotypes are shifting along with the sexual mores and gender norms that feed them.

At the beginning of *Growing Up Queer*, I explained that my objective was to explore how teenagers become sexual and gendered today by sharing what I have learned from this very particular group of kids. The youth of Spectrum are clearly products of the LGBTQ rights movement that had its origins in the 1970s. That movement established the importance of claiming a gay, lesbian, or bisexual identity and being out and proud about it. As I have argued, though, the queer movement that became prominent in the 1980s pushed back against the essentializing of identity that much of the mainstream LGBTQ rights movement has relied on. This generation of young people, regardless of their sexuality or gender, have come to understand themselves through the lens of these movements that have liberated marginalized sexuality and gender and therefore have transformed the act of becoming sexual or becoming gendered. They may not abandon identity—in fact, they seem to be proliferating it—but they also seem to be making more room for fluidity and intersectionality of identity.

In much the same spirit as the Black Lives Matter claim that, when Black people get free, everyone gets free, the youth of Spectrum have helped me to understand that when the queerest among us get free, everyone gets free. When I arrived at Spectrum for the first time so many years ago, I expected to find vulnerable young people who needed support and help, albeit not necessarily from me. I expected to be spotted as different and an outsider because of my straightness and cisgender privilege. Yet what I found were young people who hurt, yes, but who also were joyful and excited to be alive. I found a tolerance for weirdos and a community of people that nurtured each other. I learned that all of us at

Spectrum were part of becoming together, mutually constituted in the ways we self-identified, attributed identity to each other, and explored fluidity and ambiguity. I learned about the ways that queer culture has an influence that makes the mainstream better: better at doing family and better at pushing the envelope of representation. Yet Spectrum is no utopia. Within the Spectrum community, boundaries are still drawn and domination still occurs, but it has tremendous potential to imagine and manifest something better. This is what gives it so much promise.

ACKNOWLEDGMENTS

I am deeply indebted to the youth and staff of Spectrum whose contributions, support, and encouragement made this work possible. Thank you for welcoming me into your world. Know that it is with great care that I have interpreted your stories; may they ring true.

Robert Rutherford, this book is as much yours as it is mine. Thank you for always lifting me up.

I want to recognize and extend my gratitude to Jane Ward and Jessica Fields, whose generous feedback on drafts of this project were transformative. Thank you to the four anonymous reviewers who provided invaluable feedback on this manuscript.

I stand on the shoulders of many, many scholars who have come before me. While in no way a complete list, I am grateful to the following people whose thinking has most significantly influenced my work: Sara Ahmed, Judith Butler, Anne Fausto-Sterling, Roderick Ferguson, John Gagnon, Jack Halberstam, Patricia Hill Collins, Suzanne Kessler, Wendy McKenna, Jasbir Puar, Gayle Rubin, Steven Seidman, William Simon, Susan Stryker, David Valentine, Carole Vance, and Michael Warner.

A special thank you to the little-recognized lecturers, researchers, activists, and faculty whose trailblazing research and teaching on sexualities created the space for people like me to publish work and teach on these topics. I recognize that many of these individuals have been discriminated against and stigmatized in the academy because of their work in sexualities and therefore denied the opportunities that have come to me with relative ease.

Of all the valuable mentors I have had, it is to Janet Jacobs that I am the most indebted. Thank you for guiding me through this research project and for your ongoing support of me as a colleague and friend.

My thanks to the faculty who mentored me during my graduate studies at the University of Colorado Boulder, especially my advising committee: Jenn Bair, Joanne Belknap, Rob Buffington, and Eugene Walls.

Also thanks to A. J. Alejano-Steele, Matt Brown, Isaac Reed, Christi Sue, and Amy Wilkins.

Thank you to the faculty who inspired me to pursue a Ph.D. and become a professor, my mentors while I was an undergraduate student at Metropolitan State University of Denver. In particular, thanks go to Arlene Sgoutas, Anna Sampaio, Tara Tull, Jodi Wetzel, Robert Hazan, and David Sullivan.

For providing invaluable support to me throughout this process as advisers, writing partners, and dear colleagues, thanks go to Kari Alexander, Cate Bowman, Nnenia Campbell, Alison Dahl Crossley, Kimberly Dark, Emmanuel David, Tracy Deyell, Bethany Everett, Colleen Hackett, Josh LePree, Leith Lombas, Adelle Monteblanco, Naghme Naseri-Morlock, Zach Owens, Nitika Sharma, Amanda Shigihara, Julia Sinclar-Palm, Wendy Smith, and Beth Whalley.

Thank you to my colleagues and students at California State University San Marcos (CSUSM) in the Department of Sociology and Criminology and Justice Studies, in particular Kristin Bates, who turned me around when I was trying to convince myself *not* to write this book. A big thanks to graduate student assistant Dawn Lee, for helping me edit the manuscript. Thanks to the CSUSM College of Humanities, Arts, Behavioral and Social Sciences Faculty Development Committee, the CSUSM Faculty Center, and the CSUSM Department of Research and Graduate Studies for the various grants that helped me complete this work. And thank you to Robert Aiello-Hauser, Rodger D'Andreas, and Abrahán Monzón for the work you do for the CSUSM Pride and Gender Equity Centers.

I am grateful to Ilene Kalish at New York University Press for recognizing that somewhere inside of me there was a great book to be written! Thank you Maryam Arain at NYU Press for the technical support.

A very special thank you to Ellen Graham for your impeccable copyediting and content feedback and for your unflagging encouragement of me as a writer.

Thank you to my family who brought me up and have each played instrumental roles in my own becoming: my parents Sally and Joe Megeath and John Robertson; my siblings Joanie Robertson, Katy Spettel, and Andy Engelson; and my grandparents Mary Foulis Holme and Jim and Alice Holme. I send a special bit of love and adoration to those who came up behind me, my nieces and nephews Skyler, Fiona, Matilda, Na-kyia, Ethan, and Charlie.

Finally, for the cheerleading and the dance parties, much, much love to my chosen family: John Aden, Laurie Andersen, Micaela Angle, Matthew Barry, Darren Bell, Malichi Black, Laia Camps Mitchell, Erika Church, Halina Duraj, Rachel Garver, Arthur Gilkison, Dawn Greaney, Georgina Guidotti, Joe Hollins, Margaret Hollins, Lindsay Johnson, Whitney Johnson, Josh Lohmer, Becca Kuker, John Kuker, Shannan Long, Brigid McAuliffe, Rachael McGlaston Espinoza, Aleah Menefee, Bryce Merrill, Jenny Minniti-Shippey, Ben Nienass, Christopher Nelsen, Terry Nelson, Wendy Neufeld, Jody Pilmer, Rhoda Pilmer, Sean Porter, Carmen Radley, Robin Schaefer, Brandi Serpa, Jenny Schenk, Megan Shelton, Wendy Smith, Ryan Stubbs, Julie "Jet" Thompson, Trevor Trumble, Wendi Walker, Eric Walsh-Buhi, and Maggie Walsh-Buhi.

I completed a portion of this book during a writing retreat at the Dorland Mountain Arts Colony in Temecula, California.

APPENDIX

Profile of Research Participants

Pseudonym	Age	Gender Identity	Sexual Identity	Race/Ethnicity
Shane	20	Male	Gay	White
Ernie	21	Gender queer	Queer	Chicano
Brian	21	Two spirit	Queer; gay	Human/Euro
Trevor	20	Male	Gay	White American
Matthew	21	Male	Primarily gay	White
Hunter	21	No preference	Gay	Mixed
Zia	19	Gender neutral; some queer	Queer	Mixed
Red	20	Male	Other	Caucasian
Jack	18	FTM; male	Pansexual leaning towards gay male	White/hillbilly
Jamil	17	Male	Open; bisexual	Multiracial
Gabe/Kaylee	18	Androgynous	Bisexual	Native/Hispanic
Travon	16	Male	Queer	Black/Mixed
Miguel	20	Male	Gay	Mexican
Grace	21	Female	Bisexual	White
Aaron	19	Male	Gay	Mexican American/ Chicano
Isaac	19	Male	Gay	Multiracial
Alex	19	Male	Gay	White/Caucasian
Anthony	17	Male	Gay	Hispanic
Corey	18	Universal; not male or female, just me	Energy; bisexual	Mutt/mixed
Avery	19	Female	Lesbian	White
Lucy	17	Female	Lesbian	White
Lee	20	Female	Lesbian	White
Nik	18	Male; androgynous	Gay; attracted mostly to masculine guys	Caucasian
Ethan	19	Male	Straight	Biracial

(continued)

Profile of Research Participants (*cont.*)

Pseudonym	Age	Gender Identity	Sexual Identity	Race/Ethnicity
Ditto	20	Female; sometimes genderqueer	Bisexual	Biracial
William	16	Male	Gay	Multiracial/Black
Rick	19	Male; transmale	Demi-sexual	American-mutt/White
Taylor	18	Female; transfemale	Pansexual	Viking-Scandinavian
Spencer	19	n/a	n/a	n/a
Fiona	19	Female	Pansexual	White
Adam	18	Male	Gay	White
Jude	22	Female	Pansexual/Transplus	Caucasian
Jose	20	Male	Gay	Hispanic

Note: Age, gender, identity, sexual identity, and race/ethnicity are all by self-identification. More than one term indicates that the participant described themselves in multiple ways. FTM = female to male.

NOTES

INTRODUCTION

1 I use the acronym "LGBTQ" as an umbrella term to describe people who are not straight and/or cisgender identified because it seems to be the most commonly understood way to collectively describe this group. Throughout the book, while continuing to use "LGBTQ," I simultaneously problematize the various identities the acronym encompasses, the ways it conflates sexuality and gender, and the ways it conflates queerness with non-heterosexual sexualities and gender normative people.

All names of people and places in this book are pseudonyms to protect the privacy and confidentiality of the research participants.

Regarding pronouns, I asked interviewees to share their gender identity with me but did not ask what pronouns they use. I did not realize what an oversight this was until I was completing the book and found myself unsure in a few cases which pronouns a youth uses. Therefore I use the pronouns that, to the best of my memory, the youth regularly used to describe themselves and their peers in the space. While five interviewees described their gender identity as non-binary (using various terms), it was not the case that these same youths insisted that others use gender neutral pronouns to refer to them. The most common scenario among Spectrum youth who did not state a preference for a gender binary pronoun was to state that they did not care what pronouns people used to describe them. Therefore, I am fairly confident that I have used pronouns that the youths themselves would identify with, but I acknowledge that I may have erred in a few cases and offer my apologies. I discuss pronouns in much more detail in chapter 3.

2 Ghaziani (2010).

3 In her book *Queer Phenomenology*, Sara Ahmed (2006: 19) borrows a phrase from landscape architecture as a metaphor for orientation, "desire lines," which describe "unofficial paths, those marks left on the ground that show everyday comings and goings, where people deviate from the paths they are supposed to follow. . . . Such lines are indeed traces of desire; where people have taken different routes to get to this point or that point." While heterosexual desire would be an example of a path one is "supposed to follow," I'm arguing here that it still suggests choosing a path.

4 Ahmed (2006): 566.

5 Ahmed (2006): 554.
6 Waidzunas (2012): 219.
7 Savin-Williams (2005): 21.
8 Pascoe (2007): 65.
9 See Fields's (2008) ethnography of how debates over abstinence-only-before-marriage sex education versus comprehensive sex education play out across three different school districts in North Carolina. She finds that administrators and educators advocate very differently for students depending on their race and class and that sex education curriculums are heterosexist and heteronormative.
10 For more on the ways that girls, people of color, and LGBTQ-identified people often bear the brunt of sexual health interventions, see Fields (2008); and M. Fine and S. McClelland (2006).
11 For good examples of the point I am trying to make here, see Cauterucci (2016) and P. Y. Lee (2016), two editorials on the way women are held solely responsible for pregnancy in the wake of recent outbreaks of the Zika virus in Latin America.
12 Dennis Altman (1994: 508) discusses the ways that community organizations responded to the HIV/AIDS crisis in the face of neoliberal policies that privatized various services that had once been the responsibility of the state via public health departments. He states, "If the epidemic developed in a world of structural adjustments and privatization, it also developed in a world in which feminism and gay assertion meant the existence, in at least some places, of existing organizations and communities able to respond to the new crisis. The very idea that community-based organizations should play a leading role in meeting the challenge of a public health crisis is related to a whole series of political and social developments over the past twenty years." In the United States, as community organizations like LGBTQ centers responded to the HIV/AIDS crisis in the face of government neglect, these organizations became de facto experts on matters of public and sexual health. It was through the efforts of community organizations, not the government, that accurate, evidence-based information about how to prevent the spread of diseases like HIV made their way into communities.
13 Overby (2014).
14 For more on how strategic essentialism has been important to LGBTQ identity and social movements, see Gamson (1995); Seidman (1993); and Vance (1989).
15 For a concise account of how social constructionism in sociology pre-dated and therefore influenced queer theory, see Epstein (1994). See Ward (2015: 84) for a critical account of the "hegemony of bio-evolutionary accounts of sexual desire."
16 Rich (1980); Rubin (1984); and Warner (1993).
17 Ferguson (2004): 149.
18 Nagel (2003); and Stoler (1995).
19 Beyond the notion that choosing not to have children resists the straightening effects of heteronormativity, Edelman (2004) argues (largely symbolically) that refusing to reproduce is a queer act in that one refuses to perpetuate myths about a hopeful future.

20 On the least-adult role, see Mandell (1998).

21 See *Mean Girls* (2004).

22 U.S. Department of Health and Human Services (2009).

23 "Assent" is the term used to distinguish a child's agreement to participate in human subjects research from "consent," the term used to describe an adult's agreement to participate. Although the two terms are very similar in meaning, assent is not legally binding since a minor is not a legal adult.

24 U.S. Department of Health and Human Services (2009).

25 Williams (2014): 232.

26 For more on the social construction of adolescence and youth, see Best (2011); Buchholtz (2002); and Lesko (1996).

27 Waidzunas (2015); and Ward (2015).

CHAPTER 1. WELCOME TO SPECTRUM

1 When I was at Spectrum, the survey had about one hundred questions in total and was completed by youth on a computer. Although the hope on the part of the researchers was that every new visitor to Spectrum would complete a survey, this required quite a bit of diligence on the part of the staff. Therefore, completion rates were quite low. It's possible that this was a result of some resistance on the part of the staff to subject youth to research surveillance, but it also could have simply been a result of failed communication.

2 Ghaziani (2010).

3 Protection of privacy and confidentiality as determined by human subjects research protocols prevents me from identifying the name and location of the city in which I did my research and therefore prevents me from citing the source of this demographic data.

4 Dank (1971); and Plummer (1981).

5 Although many would argue that the Stonewall and Compton Lunch Counter riots in New York City and San Francisco were youth led, there was not a visible youth movement comparable to that of the Civil Rights Movement's Student Nonviolent Coordinating Committee, for example.

6 Miceli (2005).

7 See Melinda Miceli's (2005) work for a comprehensive history of LGBTQ youth organizing in the 1980s and 1990s, in particular regarding gay-straight alliances (GSAs) in schools.

8 Gibson (1989).

9 See the sociologist Tom Waidzunas's article (2012) for a complex explanation of the matter of the Gibson numbers and the resulting risk/resilience narratives about gay youth. See also Gibson (1989); Miceli (2005); Savin-Williams (2005).

10 The sociologist Tom Waidzunas (2012) uses Ian Hacking's (2006) idea of "making up people" in his thorough exploration of the rise of the gay youth suicide discourse. In order to argue that LGBTQ youth are vulnerable in society, they have to be countable, which requires a shared understanding of what defines an LGBTQ

youth. Is it based on self-identification? Identification by others? Sexual conduct? Genderqueerness? As the LGBTQ youth subject has become institutionalized in society through resources like GSAs and LGBTQ centers, for example, the very subject under investigation changes. In other words, there is a risk of essentializing sexual orientation/identity by labeling gay youth "at-risk," rather than focusing attention on the social conditions that give rise to problems like homophobic bullying.

11 Miceli (2005): 4.
12 Marx and Kettrey (2016): 1269.
13 Walls, Kane, and Wisneski (2010).
14 Kosciw et al. (2016).
15 CenterLink (n.d.).
16 Romijinders et al. (2017): 346.
17 Herdt and Boxer (1993).
18 Whittier (1994): 290.
19 Hacking (2006): 23. It is thanks to Tom Waidzunas (2012) that I discovered Hacking's article "Making Up People," which influenced my thinking here.
20 Barnes (2013); and Bumiller (2011).
21 Calmes and Baker (2012).
22 Parker-Pope (2010).
23 Markoe (2012).
24 Dvorak (2012); and Padawer (2012).
25 Although the 113th Congress passed ENDA, it never went up for a vote in the House of Representatives, as it was not expected to get the votes it needed to pass. After Congress's vote of support, President Obama signed an executive LGBT non-discrimination order that applies to federal contractors and protects federal employees. As I write this, ENDA has still not passed into federal law. In March 2017, President Trump rescinded the Fair Pay and Safe Workplaces Order, an Obama-era executive order, effectively preventing the federal government from ensuring compliance with the LGBT non-discrimination order.
26 Ford (2017).
27 Fording (2017).
28 Peters, Becker, and Davis (2017).
29 Hirschfeld Davis and Cooper (2017).
30 Southern Poverty Law Center (2017).
31 Donovan (2017).
32 Leatherby, Manibog, and Kao (2016).
33 See Lilla (2016) and Soave (2016) for discussions about the effect so-called political correctness had on the election of Donald Trump for president. To be clear, I am not arguing that it is in fact true that identity politics resulted in Trump's election. Rather, among those who voted for him, there is a pattern of expressing a strong distaste for identity politics and political correctness.
34 Schilt and Westbrook (2015).

35 Judith Halberstam (2005): 37.
36 Mary L. Gray's (2009) award-winning ethnography, *Out in the Country: Youth, Media, and Queer Visibility in Rural America*, is a good example of sociological research that complicates the urban/rural divide as relates to sexuality and youth.
37 Marantz (2017); and Penny (2017).
38 Penny (2017).
39 Marantz (2017).
40 Peters, Alter, and Grynbaum (2017).

CHAPTER 2. "THAT MAKES ME GAY"

1 Warner (1993): xxiii.
2 Ahmed (2006): 562.
3 Puar (2007): 3. Much of my analysis regarding the queer orientation of the youth of Spectrum is strongly influenced by Jasbir K. Puar's (2007) *Terrorist Assemblages: Internationalism in Queer Times*.
4 Ahmed (2006): 566.
5 This example using the non-sexual interaction with a doctor to describe sexual scripts comes from Gagnon and Simon (1973).
6 D'Augelli, Grossman, and Starks (2008); Gibson (1989); and Savin-Williams (1998).
7 Savin-Williams discusses this point in his book *The New Gay Teenager*. He attempts to clarify a variety of misleading assumptions about the origins of same-sex attraction and orientation, including the notion that gender atypical kids must be gay. He states, "Perhaps the best early *subjective* predictor of a same-sex orientation is a child's feeling of being different from peers. *Objectively*, this is usually linked to atypical gender expression. In other words, if 'inverted' in one, then 'inverted' in the other. . . . Influenced by stereotypes of their culture, adolescents with same-sex attractions come to understand that their pervasive sense that something is 'not quite right' and their acting like a tomboy or a sissy are the first signs of homosexuality" (Savin-Williams 2005: 94). He goes on to explain, as I have as well, that gender atypicality is most certainly not a universal experience of those who have same-sex attraction and orientation.
8 See Stephen Seidman's (1994) *Beyond the Closet*, where he argues that same-sex sexuality is becoming more normalized and therefore heterosexuality less compulsory. He asserts that people are more likely to identify themselves as gay, lesbian, or bisexual and less likely to conceal these identities among family, friends, and co-workers. In his book *Straights* (2015), James Dean looks specifically at how many straight women are more likely to embrace sexual fluidity and reject notions of compulsory heterosexuality, especially compared to straight men.
9 Ward (2015).
10 Ferguson (2004): 53.
11 Ferguson (2004): 149.

12 Magic: The Gathering is a trading card game, and D&D is Dungeons & Dragons, a role-playing game.

13 Warner (2000).

14 Duggan (2004): 50.

15 Warner (1993).

16 The Gay, Lesbian, and Straight Education Network (GLSEN), the leading advocacy group for LGBTQ kids in the United States, formed in 1990 and began conducting its biennial National School Climate Survey on the school-based experiences of LGBTQ youth in 1999. Prior to the 1990s and the rise of the gay-straight alliance (GSA) movement, there was virtually no acknowledgment of LGBTQ students in schools, but of course that does not mean there were no LGBTQ-identified young people prior to this time. See Miceli (2005) for more on GSAs.

17 Ward (2015): 202.

18 Seidman, Meeks, and Traschen (1999).

19 The well-known sex advice columnist and gay rights activist Dan Savage's (2015) critique of NYU Press's *description* of Jane Ward's (2015) *Not Gay* is a good example of this.

20 Diamond (2008); Waidzunas (2015); and Ward (2015).

21 Pascoe (2007).

22 Waidzunas (2015): 16.

CHAPTER 3. "LET'S BE TRANS"

1 When I was conducting fieldwork around 2010–2013, "preferred gender pronoun" was the language being used in queer spaces like Spectrum. Since then, it has become more acceptable to drop the "preferred" part, as it suggests one's gender is somehow inauthentic. I've chosen to use "preferred" in my account since it is consistent with what was happening at the time.

2 Ahmed (2006): 60.

3 Butler (2004): 216.

4 Butler (2004): 217.

5 Muñoz (2009): 185.

6 Stryker (2006): 9.

7 Serano (2007); Stryker (2007); and Stryker and Currah (2014).

8 Dean (2015): 249.

9 Each of the following three readings are nuanced discussions about the intertwining relationship between gender and sexuality: Gagné, Tewksbury, and McGaughey (1997); Valentine (2004); and Vidal-Ortiz (2002).

10 As Valentine (2007) explains, the term "transgender" was not widely in use until the mid-1990s in the United States. Therefore, the use of this term to describe children is a new phenomenon. See Meadow (2011, 2018) and Travers (2018) for more on the experiences of parents raising transgender, gender non-conforming, and genderqueer kids.

11 Dvorak (2012); and Padawer (2012).

12 Walsh (2015).

13 Petrusich (2015).

14 Kessler and McKenna (1978).

15 Kessler and McKenna (1978).

16 One of the reviewers of this book commented that she was surprised at these findings since her gender studies students are very adept at using gender neutral pronouns. While I think there are certain geographical and cultural locations where the use of gender neutral pronouns are becoming more common, my research leads me to believe that these places remain exceptions to the norm in the United States.

17 Lucal (1999): 785.

18 For more on the pathologizing of trans*, see Bryant (2008); Butler (2004); Irvine (1990); Mason-Shrock (1996); and Stone (1991).

19 Parekh (2016), citing American Psychiatric Association (2013).

20 The Parable of the Lamp is found in three of the New Testament gospels, Matthew 5:14–15, Mark 4:21–25, and Luke 8:16–18.

21 Butler (1990).

22 Lucal (1999): 791.

23 In my interviews with youth who identified as transgender, I intentionally did not press for information about surgeries, medical treatments, or hormone therapies because I felt that doing so would reinforce existing ideas about who is and is not a legitimate trans* person. Some participants disclosed this information to me, and at times I mention these details when I think it's contextually important, but it was not the case that among the people I interviewed being trans* also meant taking hormones or having surgeries. I approached this matter from the perspective described by the critical studies scholar Julian Carter (2014: 235), who discusses the term "transition" for *TSQ: Transgender Studies Quarterly*: "Many North American trans-communities insist that 'everyone transitions in their own way': open-ended refusal to define 'transition' is a principled stance against institutionalizing any given form of trans-being. Such resistance reflects decades of struggle over who decides what counts as legitimate trans-/gender expression—struggle that clings to the word itself." Therefore, when I talk about gender attribution and how secondary and tertiary sex characteristics play a role in how we interpret each other's gender, I'm not concerned with *how* a person came by these characteristics but, rather, how they function in the attribution process.

24 Hormone replacement therapies involve prescribing hormones or hormone blockers to people for a variety of different reasons. For transgender people, hormone replacement therapy is a form of gender confirming healthcare that can alter the effects of secondary sex characteristics in order to align with one's gender identity.

25 For more on being genderqueer or gender ambiguous, while not feeling as if one is the "wrong" gender or wanting to change gender, see Devor's (1989) concept

of "gender bending," Judith Halberstam's (1998) "female masculinity," and Lucal's (1999) personal experience of embodying gender ambiguity.

26 See Davidson (2007) for a smart and concise discussion of the ways in which the term "transgender," as an umbrella term, is understood within the trans* community. In particular, Davidson addresses some of the contestation between those people who have transitioned from one gender to another (transbinary) and those who embrace gender fluidity and non-binary gender.

27 Spade (2011): 152.

28 In October 2017, the State of California became the first to allow a non-binary gender option on birth certificates. Both Washington and Oregon have non-binary gender options on driver's licenses.

29 Westbrook and Schilt (2013).

30 Schilt and Westbrook (2009).

31 North Carolina General Assembly (2016).

32 U.S. Department of Justice (2016).

33 Schilt and Westbrook (2009).

34 David Valentine (2004) troubles the relationship between sexuality and gender as categories showing how once we assign a label to an experience, there is a risk that the label becomes the fact, not the experience. He is pointing to the difference between a theoretical separation of gender and sexuality—often in the service of social justice activism, academic research, and service provision—and the actual lived experience of one's gender and sexuality, which is interwoven. Valentine suggests there is some risk in society's increasing emphasis on gender identity. How much do the categories—often created to describe others—come to subsume people's lived experience of their sexualities and/or genders? Further, whose genders and sexualities get erased in the process of categorization?

CHAPTER 4. "GOOGLE KNOWS EVERYTHING"

1 Weinrich (1997): 62.

2 For a sampling of various empirical studies and theoretical analyses on this topic, see Bryson (2007); Craig et al. (2015); Gray (2009); Jack J. Halberstam (2012a); Muise (2011); Saraswati (2013); Stryker (2008); and Weinrich (1997).

3 Pascoe (2011). See also Craig et al. (2015).

4 Charmaraman and McKamey (2011) used focus groups with urban-based youth to learn about sexuality and relationships. Media was found to be a common and influential way that youth were exposed to and learned about sexuality.

5 Prensky (2001).

6 Döring (2009); and Weber, Quiring, and Dauschmann (2012).

7 Weber, Quiring, and Dauschmann (2012): 410.

8 Pascoe (2011).

9 Goffman (1959).

10 Gagnon and Simon (1973).

11 Gagnon (2004): 118.

12 Gagnon (2004): 125.
13 Green (2008): 605.
14 Green (2008): 606.
15 Fejes and Petrich (1993); and Keilwasser and Wolf (1992).
16 Sedgwick (1991).
17 Russo (1981): 27.
18 Russo (1981): 30.
19 G. Black (1994).
20 G. Black (1994).
21 *Silence of the Lambs* (1991).
22 Russo (1981): 52.
23 Avila-Saavedra (2009).
24 Avila-Saavedra (2009); and Kanner (2003).
25 Jack J. Halberstam (2012a): xix.
26 Napier (2005).
27 Roncero-Menendez (2014).
28 Hall (2010).
29 *Cartoon Network Wiki* (n.d.); and *Anime Savvy* (2010).
30 Roncero-Menendez (2014).
31 The closest U.S. equivalent to the Japanese host/hostess bar might be a strip club, but host club workers do not typically engage in nudity, dancing, or sex acts inside the clubs; they play the role of chaperone while entertaining their upscale clients and, most important, getting them to spend as much money as possible while in the club. *Ouran High School Host Club* is not a depiction of high schoolers engaging in sex work; rather, the host club is a social space where the wealthy girls of Ouran High go for fun and to flirt with boys.
32 *InuYasha Wiki* (n.d.).
33 Napier (2005): 13.
34 Napier (2005).
35 Rowling (1997–2007).
36 R. Black (2008): 13.
37 Collins (2008–2010); Meyer (2005–2008); and Rowling (1997–2007).
38 Thorn (2004): 183.
39 R. Black (2008); Busse (2005); Jenkins (1992); Kustritz (2003); Scodari and Felder (2000); and Somogyi (2002).
40 Jenkins (1992): 219.
41 Thorn (2004): 179.
42 Mizoguchi (2010): 159.
43 Welker (2006): 866.

CHAPTER 5. "IT'S GOING TO BE OKAY"

1 In her work examining the social construction of the pedophile and its relationship to shoring up the patriarchal family, Elise Chenier (2012: 174) claims, "In the

modern western state, the family is ground zero for sexual normalization." See also Ferguson (2004); and Stoler (1995).

2 D. Smith (1993).

3 Stacey (1993): 545.

4 Hill Collins (1994); Neubeck and Cazenave (2001); D. Roberts (2002); and Stoler (1995).

5 The Moynihan Report is a 1965 report published by the then assistant secretary of labor Daniel Patrick Moynihan, titled *The Negro Family: The Case for National Action*. Moynihan's objective was to convince Congress that civil rights legislation by itself would not solve the problem of racial inequality, arguing that some of the causes of inequality could be found within the structure of the Black family itself. The Moynihan Report has been a source of fierce debate since it was published, one of the strongest critiques being that it blames the Black family for problems that are in fact institutionalized in U.S. society. See Geary (2015) for an annotated edition of the Report published in the *Atlantic*.

6 Bennett and Battle (2001): 56.

7 See Ferguson (2004).

8 For more on ways that heteropatriarchal family formation makes women and children vulnerable to violence and reinforces gender norms, see Chenier (2012); Gordon (1988); Kaye (2005); and Stacey (1993).

9 See Moore's (2011) work on gay Black women, in particular her discussion of the recent shift among Black people to live openly as gay, which Moore argues is resulting in shifting norms around homosexuality in Black communities. See also Weston (1991).

10 See Weston (1991) on LGBTQ kinship. For more on shifting norms regarding same-sex parents and families, see Biblarz, Carroll, and Burke (2014).

11 Martin et al. (2009); and Savin-Williams and Dubé (1998).

12 D'Augelli, Grossman, and Starks (2008); Gibson (1989); Herdt (1989); Savin-Williams (1998); and Troiden (1989).

13 See Savin-Williams (2001) for a complex analysis of problems with the data on sexual minorities and suicide, in particular his discussion of the "suffering suicidal" script.

14 The reader should understand that I am primarily referring here to the coming-out experiences of sexual-minority youths, and this discussion does not necessarily reflect the experiences of young people coming out to their parents as transgender.

15 The gender atypical children in question do not include trans-identified youths but, rather, cisgender youths whose gender expression and presentation marks them as atypical males or atypical females. See D'Augelli, Grossman, and Starks (2005).

16 Savin-Williams (2005).

17 D'Augelli, Grossman, and Starks (2005); and Savin-Williams and Dubé (1998).

18 Seidman, Meeks, and Traschen (1999).

19 Stacey and Biblarz (2001).
20 Judith Halberstam (2005): 40.
21 Moore (2011).
22 Newman and Muzzonigro (1993).
23 Edin and Kefalas (2005); and Fields (2001).
24 Fields (2001).
25 Fields (2001).
26 Jack J. Halberstam (2012a): 58.

CONCLUSION

1 Fausto-Sterling (1993, 2000b); E. Stein (1999); and Wade (2013).
2 Hill Collins (1990).
3 Schwartz (2012): 13.
4 Schwartz (2012): 43.
5 Jack J. Halberstam (2012b).
6 Jack J. Halberstam (2012a): 26.
7 Jack J. Halberstam (2012a): 81.
8 In October of 2017, the State of California became the first to allow a non-binary gender option on birth certificates. Both Washington and Oregon have non-binary gender options on driver's licenses. For more on how institutions regulate gender, see Currah and Mulqueen (2011); Fogg Davis (2017); and Spade (2011).
9 Preston and Cushman (2012).
10 In "Thinking Sex: Notes for a Radical Theory of the Politics of Sexuality," Gayle Rubin (1984: 13) describes a hierarchy of sexual value in which "good, normal, natural, and blessed" sexuality—like heterosexuality, monogamy, reproductive sex, and vanilla sex—resides within the "charmed circle," while "bad, abnormal, unnatural, and damned" sexuality—like homosexuality, promiscuity, unmarried sex, and sadomasochistic sex—resides in the "outer limits."
11 For more on whiteness and the color line, see Gans (1999); J. Lee and F. Bean (2004); and Steinberg (2004).
12 Duggan (2004); Ferguson (2004); and Puar (2005).
13 For a particularly surprising look at some of the ways the state compels asylum seekers to prove their sexual identities, see Rachel A. Lewis's (2014) *Sexualities* article.
14 See the concluding chapter in Waidzunas (2015), in which, based on his research in Uganda, he makes a compelling argument for rethinking the way human rights agendas frame sexual orientation.
15 In her book *Respectably Queer*, Jane Ward (2008: 149) calls for "a movement-based return to ethics" and a rejection of profit-motivated calls for equality.
16 Gilmore (2007); Rodríguez (2007); and Spade (2011).
17 Ahmed (2006): 570.
18 Black Lives Matter (2017a).
19 Black Lives Matter (2017b).

20 Stryker (2008): 150.

21 Stryker (2008): 150. See also Spade (2011).

22 These are common stereotypes or myths that circulate within the LGBTQ community, so common, in fact, that the young people in our discussion group had no problem identifying them when prompted. A colloquial reference to research similar to that found in *American Couples: Money, Work, Sex* by the sociologists Philip Blumstein and Pepper Schwartz (1983) suggests that women in long-term lesbian relationships tended toward being less sexually active than other couple formations. The notion of lesbian bed death has been criticized for being a myth and not truly representative of lesbian intimacy. In contrast, gay men are portrayed in the popular imagination as hypersexual partiers who use drugs to intensify sex. Again, while there is no denying that sex and partying are components of gay male culture, they are not actually representative of all gay men. Finally, stereotypes of transgender people often result in either hypersexualization—as in the transwoman sex worker—or asexualization—the idea that trans people are not sexually desirable.

BIBLIOGRAPHY

Ahmed, Sara. 2006. *Queer Phenomenology: Orientations, Objects, Others.* Durham, NC: Duke University Press.

Altman, Dennis. 1994. "The Emergence of a Non-governmental Response to AIDS." In *Social Perspectives in Lesbian and Gay Studies*, edited by Peter M. Nardi and Beth E. Schneider, 506–520. London: Routledge.

American Psychiatric Association. 2013. *Diagnostic and Statistical Manual of Mental Disorders*, 5th ed. Washington, DC: American Psychiatric Association.

Anime Savvy. 2010. "The History of Anime and Its Arrival in America," June 29. https://animesavvy.wordpress.com.

Avila-Saavedra, Guillermo. 2009. "Nothing Queer about Queer Television: Televised Construction of Gay Masculinities." *Media, Culture and Society* 31(1): 5–21.

Banerjee, Sarbani, and Amitra Hodge. 2007. "Internet Usage: A within Race Analysis." *Race, Gender and Class* 14(3/4): 228–246.

Barnes, Robert. 2013. "Supreme Court Strikes Down Key Part of Defense of Marriage Act." *Washington Post*, June 26. www.washingtonpost.com.

Bay-Cheng, Laina Y. 2005. "Left to Their Own Devices: Disciplining Youth Discourse on Sexuality Education Electronic Bulletin Boards." *Sexuality Research and Social Policy* 2(1): 37–50.

Beaty, Lee A. 1999. "Identity Development of Homosexual Youth and Parental and Familial Influences on the Coming Out Process." *Adolescence* 34 (Fall): 597–601.

Bennett, Michael, and Juan Battle. 2001. "'We Can See Them, But We Can't Hear Them': LGBT Members of African American Families." In *Queer Families, Queer Politics: Challenging Culture and the State*, edited by Mary Bernstein and Renate Reimann, 53–67. New York: Columbia University Press.

Berger, Alan S., William Simon, and John H. Gagnon. 1973. "Youth and Pornography in Social Context." *Archives of Sexual Behavior* 2(4): 279–308.

Best, Amy. 2011. "Youth Identity Formation: Contemporary Identity Work." *Sociology Compass* 5(10): 908–922.

Biblarz, Timothy J., Megan Carroll, and Nathaniel Burke. 2014. "Same-Sex Families." In *The Wiley-Blackwell Companion to the Sociology of Families*, edited by Judith Treas, Jacqueline Scott, and Martin Richards, 109–131. Oxford: John Wiley & Sons.

The Bird Cage. 1996. Film, directed by Mike Nichols, written by Elaine May. Beverly Hills, CA: United Artists.

Birkett, Michelle, Dorothy L. Espelage, and Brian Koenig. 2009. "LGB and Questioning Students in Schools: The Moderating Effects of Homophobic Bullying and School Climate on Negative Outcomes." *Journal of Youth and Adolescence* 38(7): 989–1000.

Black, Gregory D. 1994. *Hollywood Censored: Morality Codes, Catholics, and the Movies*. Cambridge: Cambridge University Press.

Black, Rebecca W. 2008. *Adolescents and Online Fan Fiction*. New York: Peter Lang.

Black Lives Matter. 2017a. "Herstory." https://blacklivesmatter.com.

Black Lives Matter. 2017b. "What We Believe." https://blacklivesmatter.com.

Blumer, Herbert. 1969. *Symbolic Interactionism: Perspective and Method*. Berkeley: University of California Press.

Blumstein, Philip, and Pepper Schwartz. 1983. *American Couples: Money, Work, Sex*. New York: William Morrow & Co.

Brill, Stephanie, and Rachel Pepper. 2008. *The Transgender Child: A Handbook for Families and Professionals*. San Francisco, CA: Cleis Press.

Brokeback Mountain. 2005. Film, directed by Ang Lee, written by Larry McMurtry and Diana Ossana. Universal City, CA: Focus Features.

Brown, Jane D., and Sarah N. Keller. 2000. "Can the Mass Media be Healthy Sex Educators?" *Forum* 32(5): 255–256.

Bryant, Karl. 2008. "In Defense of Gay Children: 'Progay' Homophobia and the Production of Homonormativity." *Sexualities* 11(4): 455–475.

Bryson, Mary. 2007. "When Jill Jacks In: Queer Women and the Net." *Feminist Media Studies* 4(3): 239–254.

Buchholtz, Mary. 2002. "Youth and Cultural Practice." *Annual Review of Anthropology* 31: 525–52.

Buffy the Vampire Slayer. 1997–2003. Television show. Los Angeles: 20th Television.

Bumiller, Elisabeth. 2011. "Obama Ends 'Don't Ask, Don't Tell' Policy." *New York Times*, July 22. www.nytimes.com.

Busse, Kristina. 2005. "Digital Get Down: Postmodern Boy Band Slash and the Queer Female Space." In *Eroticism in American Culture*, edited by Cheryl Malcolm and Jopi Nyman, 103–125. Gdansk: Gdansk University Press.

Butler, Judith. 1990. *Gender Trouble*. New York: Routledge.

———. 2004. *Undoing Gender*. New York: Routledge.

Calmes, Jackie, and Peter Baker. 2012. "Obama Says Same-Sex Marriage Should Be Legal." *New York Times*, May 9. www.nytimes.com.

Calzo, Jerel P., Toni C. Antonucci, Vicki M. Mays, and Susan D. Cochran. 2011. "Retrospective Recall of Sexual Orientation Identity Development among Gay, Lesbian, and Bisexual Adults." *Developmental Psychology* 47(6): 1658–1673.

Carter, Julian. 2014. "Transition." *TSQ: Transgender Studies Quarterly* 1(1–2): 235–237.

Cartoon Network Wiki. n.d. "Sailor Moon." http://cartoonnetwork.wikia.com.

Cass, Vivienne C. 1979. "Homosexual Identity Formation: A Theoretical Model." *Journal of Homosexuality* 4(3): 219–235.

Cauterucci, Christina. 2016. "Why Aren't Governments Telling Men to Prevent Zika Pregnancies, Too?" *Slate*, February 4. www.slate.com.

CenterLink. n.d. "CenterLink LGBT Community Center Member Directory." www. lgbtcenters.org.

Centers for Disease Control and Prevention. 2011. "Trends in the Prevalence of Sexual Behaviors and HIV Testing, National YRBS [Youth Risk Behavior Survey]: 1991–2011." National Center for HIV/AIDS, Viral Hepatitis, STD, and TB Prevention, Division of Adolescent and School Health. Washington, DC: Centers for Disease Control and Prevention. www.cdc.gov.

Charmaraman, Linda, and Corinne McKamey. 2011. "Urban Early Adolescent Narratives on Sexuality: Accidental and Intentional Influences of Family, Peers, and the Media." *Sexuality Research and Social Policy* 8(4): 253–266.

Chenier, Elise. 2012. "The Natural Order of Disorder: Pedophilia, Stranger Danger and the Normalising Family." *Sexuality and Culture* 16: 172–186.

Cillizza, Chris, and Sean Sullivan. 2013. "How Proposition 8 Passed in California—and Why It Wouldn't Today." *Washington Post*, March 26. www.washingtonpost.com.

Coleman, Eli. 1982. "Developmental Stages of the Coming Out Process." *Journal of Homosexuality* 4(2–3): 219–235.

Collins, Suzanne. 2008–2010. *The Hunger Games* trilogy. New York: Scholastic.

Connell, R. W. 1992. "A Very Straight Gay: Masculinity, Homosexual Experience, and the Dynamics of Gender." *American Sociological Review* 57(6): 735–751.

———. 1995. *Masculinities*. Berkeley: University of California Press.

Craig, Shelley L., Lauren McInroy, Lance T. McCready, and Ramona Alaggia. 2015. "Media: A Catalyst for Resilience in Lesbian, Gay Bisexual, Transgender, and Queer Youth." *Journal of LGBT Youth* 12(3): 254–275.

Currah, Paisley, and Tara Mulqueen. 2011. "Securitizing Gender: Identity, Biometrics, and Transgender Bodies at the Airport." *Social Research* 78(2): 557–582.

Dank, Barry M. 1971. "Coming Out in the Gay World." *Psychiatry* 34: 180–197.

D'Augelli, Anthony, Arnold H. Grossman, and Michael T. Starks. 2005. "Parents' Awareness of Lesbian, Gay, and Bisexual Youths' Sexual Orientation." *Journal of Marriage and Family* 67(May): 474–482.

———. 2008. "Families of Gay, Lesbian, and Bisexual Youth: What Do Parents and Siblings Know and How Do They React?" *Journal of LGBT Family Studies* 4(1): 95–115.

D'Augelli, Anthony R., and Scott L. Hershberger. 1993. "Lesbian, Gay, and Bisexual Youth in Community Settings: Personal Challenges and Mental Health Problems." *American Journal of Community Psychology* 21(4): 421–448.

Davidson, Megan. 2007. "Seeking Refuge under the Umbrella: Inclusion, Exclusion, and Organizing within the Category *Transgender*." *Sexuality Research and Social Policy: Journal of NSRC* 4(4): 60–80.

Dawson's Creek. 1998–2003. Television show. Culver City, CA: Sony Pictures Television.

Dean, James. 2015. *Straights: Heterosexuality in Post-closeted Culture*. New York: New York University Press.

Devor, Holly. 1989. *Gender Blending: Confronting the Limits of Duality*. Bloomington: University of Indiana Press.

Diamond, Lisa M. 2005. "What We Got Wrong about Sexual Identity Development: Unexpected Findings from a Longitudinal Study of Young Women." In *Sexual Orientation and Mental Health: Examining Identity and Development in Lesbian, Gay, and Bisexual People*, edited by Allen M. Omoto and Howard S. Kurtzman, 73–94. Washington, DC: American Psychological Association Press.

———. 2008. *Sexual Fluidity: Understanding Women's Love and Desire.* Cambridge, MA: Harvard University Press.

Doctor Who. 2005–present. Television show. New York: BBC America.

Donovan, Megan K. 2017. "The Looming Threat to Sex Education: A Resurgence of Federal Funding for Abstinence-Only Programs." *Guttmacher Policy Review* 20: 44–47.

Döring, Nicola M. 2009. "The Internet's Impact on Sexuality: A Critical Review of 15 Years of Research." *Computers in Human Behavior* 25(5): 1089–1101.

Dubé, Eric M., and Ritch C. Savin-Williams. 1999. "Sexual Identity Development among Ethnic Sexual-Minority Male Youths." *Developmental Psychology* 35(6): 1389–1398.

Duggan, Lisa. 2004. *The Twilight of Equality? Neoliberalism, Cultural Politics, and the Attack on Democracy.* Boston: Beacon Press.

Dvorak, Petula. 2012. "Transgender at 5." *Washington Post,* May 19. www.washingtonpost.com.

Edelman, Lee. 2004. *No Future: Queer Theory and the Death Drive.* Durham, NC: Duke University Press.

Edin, Kathryn, and Maria Kefalas. 2005. *Promises I Can Keep: Why Poor Women Put Motherhood before Marriage.* Berkeley: University of California Press.

Eliason, Mickey. 2011. "Introduction to Special Issue on Suicide, Mental Health, and Youth Development." *Journal of Homosexuality* 58(1): 4–9.

Epstein, Steven. 1994. "A Queer Encounter: Sociology and the Study of Sexuality." *Sociological Theory* 12(2): 188–202.

Eyre, Stephen L., Rebecca de Guzman, Amy A. Donovan, and Calvin Boissiere. 2004. "'Hormones Is Not Magic Wands': Ethnography of a Transgender Scene in Oakland, California." *Ethnography* 5(2): 147–172.

Fausto-Sterling, Anne. 1993. "The Five Sexes." *Sciences* 33(2): 20.

———. 2000a. "Gender Systems: Toward a Theory of Human Sexuality" in *Sexing the Body: Gender Politics and the Construction of Sexuality,* 1st ed. New York: Basic Books.

———. 2000b. "The Five Sexes Revisited." *Sciences* 40(4): 18.

Fejes, Fred, and Kevin Petrich. 1993. "Invisibility, Homophobia and Heterosexism: Lesbians, Gays and the Media." *Critical Studies in Mass Communication* 10: 396–422.

Felicity. 1998–2002. Television show. Burbank, CA: Buena Vista Television.

Ferguson, Roderick A. 2004. *Aberrations in Black: Toward a Queer of Color Critique.* Minneapolis: University of Minnesota Press.

Fields, Jessica. 2001. "Normal Queers: Straight Parents Respond to Their Children's 'Coming Out.'" *Symbolic Interaction* 24(2): 165–187.

———. 2008. *Risky Lessons: Sex Education and Social Inequality*. New Brunswick, NJ: Rutgers University Press.

Fine, Gary Alan. 2004. "Adolescence as Cultural Toolkit: High School Debate and the Repertoires of Childhood and Adulthood." *Sociological Quarterly* 45(1): 1–20.

Fine, Michelle, and Sara I. McClelland. 2006. "Sexuality Education and Desire: Still Missing after All These Years." *Harvard Educational Review* 76(3): 297–338.

Floyd, Frank J., and Terry S. Stein. 2002. "Sexual Orientation Identity Formation among Gay, Lesbian and Bisexual Youths: Multiple Patterns of Milestone." *Journal of Research on Adolescence* 12(2): 167–191.

Fogg Davis, Heath. 2017. *Beyond Trans: Does Gender Matter?* New York: New York University Press.

Ford, Matt. 2017. "Trump Nominates Neil Gorsuch for the U.S. Supreme Court." *Atlantic*, January 31. www.theatlantic.com.

Fording, Richard. 2017. "Commentary: Five Myths about Jeff Sessions." *Chicago Tribune*, January 20. www.chicagotribune.com.

The Fosters. 2013–present. Television show. Los Angeles: Nuyorican Productions.

Foucault, Michel. 1990. *History of Sexuality: An Introduction*, vol. 1. New York: Vintage Books.

Freud, Sigmund. 1962. *Three Essays on the Theory of Sexuality*. Translated by James Strachey. New York: Basic Books.

Friedman, Mark S., Anthony J. Silvestre, Melanie A. Gold, Nina Markovic, Ritch C. Savin-Williams, James Huggins, and Randal L. Sell. 2004. "Adolescents Define Sexual Orientation and Suggest Ways to Measure It." *Journal of Adolescence* 27(3): 303–317.

Gagné, Patricia, Richard Tewksbury, and Deanna McGaughey. 1997. "Coming Out and Crossing Over: Identity Formation and Proclamation in a Transgender Community." *Gender and Society* 11(4): 478–508.

Gagnon, John H. 2004. *An Interpretation of Desire: Essays in the Study of Sexuality*. Chicago: University of Chicago Press.

Gagnon, John H., and William Simon. 1973. *Sexual Conduct: The Social Sources of Human Sexuality*. Chicago: Aldine.

Gamson, Joshua. 1995. "Must Identity Movements Self-Destruct? A Queer Dilemma." *Social Problems* 42(3): 390–407.

Gans, Herbert J. 1999. "The Possibility of a New Racial Hierarchy in the Twenty-First Century United States." In *Cultural Territories of Race: Black and White Boundaries*, edited by Michéle Lamont, 371–391. Chicago: University of Chicago Press.

Garnets, Linda, and Douglas Kimmel. 1991. "Lesbian and Gay Male Dimensions in the Psychological Study of Human Diversity." In *Psychological Perspectives on Human Diversity in America*, edited by Jacqueline D. Goodchilds, 143–192. Washington, DC: American Psychological Association.

Gattis, Maurice N. 2009. "Psychosocial Problems Associated with Homelessness in Sexual Minority Youths." *Journal of Human Behavior in the Social Environment* 19(8): 1066–1094.

Geary, Daniel. 2015. "The Moynihan Report: An Annotated Edition." *Atlantic*, September 14. www.theatlantic.com.

Ghaziani, Amin. 2010. "There Goes the Gayborhood?" *Contexts* 9(3): 64–66.

Gibson, Paul. 1989. "Gay Male and Lesbian Youth Suicide." *United States Department of Health and Human Services Report to the Secretary's Task Force on Youth Suicide*. Washington DC: U.S. Department of Health and Human Services.

Gilmore, Ruth Wilson. 2007. *Golden Gulag: Prisons, Surplus, Crisis, and Opposition* Berkeley: University of California Press.

Glee. 2009–2015. Television show. Los Angeles: 20th Television.

Glover, Jenna A., Renee V. Galliher, and Trenton G. Lamere. 2009. "Identity Development and Exploration among Sexual Minority Adolescents: Examination of a Multidimensional Model." *Journal of Homosexuality* 56(1): 77–101.

Goffman, Erving. 1959. *The Presentation of Self in Everyday Life*. New York: Anchor Books.

Goodyear, Sarah. 2014. "The Particular Challenge of Helping Homeless LGBTQ Youth." *CityLab*, January 27. www.citylab.com.

Gordon, Linda. 1988. "The Politics of Child Sexual Abuse: Notes from American History." *Feminist Review* 28: 56–64.

Gray, Mary L. 2009. *Out in the Country: Youth, Media, and Queer Visibility in Rural America*. New York: New York University Press.

Green, Adam Isaiah. 2008. "Erotic Habitus: Toward a Sociology of Desire." *Theory and Society* 37: 597–626.

Hacking, Ian. 2006. "Making Up People." *London Review of Books*, August 17, 2006.

Halberstam, Jack J. 2012a. *Gaga Feminism: Sex, Gender, and the End of Normal*. Boston: Beacon Press.

———. 2012b. "On Pronouns" Jack Halberstam (blog), September 3. www.jackhalberstam.com.

Halberstam, Judith. 1998. *Female Masculinity*. Durham, NC: Duke University Press.

———. 2005. *In a Queer Time and Place: Transgender Bodies, Subcultural Lives*. New York: New York University Press.

Hale, Jacob. n.d. "Suggested Rules for Non-transexuals Writing about Transexuals, Transexuality, Transsexualism, or Trans_____." Hosted at Sandy Stone's personal website, *Sandy Stone!* https://sandystone.com.

Hall, Alexis. 2010. "Gay or Gei? Reading 'Realness' in Japanese Yaoi Manga." In *Boy's Love Manga: Essays on the Sexual Ambiguity and Cross-Cultural Fandom of the Genre*, edited by Antonia Levi, Mark McHarry, and Dru Pagliassotti, 211–220. Jefferson, NC: McFarland.

Hammack, Phillip L., Elizabeth Morgan Thompson, and Andrew Pilecki. 2009. "Configurations of Identity among Sexual Minority Youth: Context, Desire, and Narrative." *Journal of Youth and Adolescence* 38: 867–883.

Haussmen, Bernice L. 2001. "Recent Transgender Theory." *Feminist Studies* 27(2): 465–490.

Herdt, Gilbert. 1989. "Gay and Lesbian Youth: Emergent Identities and Cultural Scenes at Home and Abroad." *Journal of Homosexuality* 17(1/2): 1–41.

Herdt, Gilbert, and Andrew Boxer. 1993. *The Children of Horizons: How Gay and Lesbian Teens Are Leading a New Way Out of the Closet*. Boston: Beacon Press.

Hill Collins, Patricia. 1990. *Black Feminist Thought: Knowledge, Consciousness, and the Politics of Empowerment* Boston: Unwin Hyman.

———. 1994. *Black Sexual Politics: African Americans, Gender, and the New Racism* New York: Routledge.

Hirschfeld Davis, Julie, and Helene Cooper. 2017. "Trump Says Transgender People Will Not Be Allowed in the Military." *New York Times*, July 26. www.nytimes.com.

InuYasha Wiki. n.d. "Jakotsu." http://inuyasha.wikia.com. This website is part of the overall *Fandom* website at http://fandom.wikia.com.

Irvine, Janice. 1990. *Disorders of Desire: Sex and Gender in Modern American Sexology*. Philadelphia: Temple University Press.

Jamil, Omar B., Gary W. Harper, and Isabele M. Fernandez. 2009. "Sexual and Ethnic Identity Development among Gay-Bisexual-Questioning (GBQ) Male Ethnic Minority Adolescents." *Cultural Diversity and Ethnic Minority Psychology* 15(3): 203–214.

Jenkins, Henry. 1992. *Textual Poachers: Television, Fans, and Participatory Culture*. New York: Routledge.

Kane, Emily. 2006. "No Way My Boys Are Going to Be like That!' Parents' Responses to Children's Gender Nonconformity." *Gender and Society* 20(2): 149–176.

Kanner, Melinda. 2003. "Can *Will & Grace* Be 'Queered'?" *Gay and Lesbian Review Worldwide* 10(4): 34–36.

Katz, Jonathan Ned. 2007. *The Invention of Heterosexuality*. Chicago: University of Chicago Press.

Kaye, Kerwin. 2005. "Sexual Abuse Victims and the Wholesome Family: Feminist, Psychological, and State Discourses." In *Regulating Sex: The Politics of Intimacy and Identity*, edited by Elizabeth Bernstein and Laurie Schaffner, 143–166. New York: Routledge.

Kielwasser, Alfred P., and Michelle A. Wolf. 1992. "Mainstream Television, Adolescent Homosexuality, and Significant Silence." *Critical Studies in Mass Communication* 9: 350–373.

Kendall, Nancy. 2008. "The State(s) of Sexuality Education in America." *Sexuality Research and Social Policy: Journal of NSRC* 5(2): 1–11.

Kessler, Suzanne J. 1998. *Lessons from the Intersexed*. New Brunswick, NJ: Rutgers University Press.

Kessler, Suzanne J., and Wendy McKenna. 1978. *Gender: An Ethnomethodological Approach*. Chicago: University of Chicago Press.

Kinsey, Alfred C., Wardell B. Pomeroy, and Clyde E. Martin. 1948. *Sexual Behavior in the Human Male*. Philadelphia: Saunders.

Kosciw, Joseph G., Emily A. Greytak, and Elizabeth M. Diaz. 2009. "Who, What, Where, When, and Why: Demographic and Ecological Factors Contributing to Hostile School Climate for Lesbian, Gay, Bisexual, and Transgender Youth." *Journal of Youth and Adolescence* 38(7): 976–988.

Kosciw, Joseph G., Emily A. Greytak, Noreen M. Giga, Christian Villenas, and David J. Danischewski. 2016. "The 2015 National School Climate Survey." New York: The Gay, Lesbian, and Straight Education Network. www.glsen.org.

Kruks, Gabe. 1991. "Gay and Lesbian Homeless/Street Youth: Special Issues and Concerns." *Journal of Adolescent Health* 12(7): 515–518.

Kustritz, Anne. 2003. "Slashing the Romance Narrative." *Journal of American Culture.* 26(3): 371–384.

Leatherby, Lauren, Clair Manibog, and Joanna Kao. 2016. "Trump's Victory Explained in 8 Charts." *Financial Times,* November 16. www.ft.com.

Lee, Jennifer, and Frank D. Bean. 2004. "America's Changing Color Lines: Immigration, Race/ Ethnicity, and Multiracial Identification." *Annual Review of Sociology* 30: 221–242.

Lee, Paula Young. 2016. "Zika Virus Warnings: Once Again, the Burden of Sexual and Reproductive Accountability Falls Squarely (and Solely) on Women." *Dame Magazine,* February 3. www.damemagazine.com.

Lenhart, Amanda. 2013. "Young Adults, Mobile Phones, and Social Media: Technology and the Transition to Adulthood." Pew Research Center, May 7. www.pewinternet.org.

Lesko, Nancy. 1996. "Denaturalizing Adolescence: The Politics of Contemporary Representations" *Youth and Society* 28(2): 139–161.

Lewis, Rachel A. 2014. "'Gay? Prove It': The Politics of Queer Anti-deportation Activism." *Sexualities* 17(8): 958–975.

Lilla, Mark. 2016. "The End of Identity Liberalism." *New York Times,* November 18. www.nytimes.com.

Lorber, Judith. 1994. *Paradoxes of Gender.* New Haven, CT: Yale University Press.

Lucal, Betsy. 1999. "What It Means to Be Gendered Me: Life on the Boundaries of a Dichotomous Gender System." *Gender and Society* 13(6): 781–797.

The L Word. 2004–2006. Television show. New York: Showtime.

Mandell, Nancy. 1988. "The Least-Adult Role in Studying Children." *Journal of Contemporary Ethnography* 16(4): 433–467.

Marantz, Andrew. 2017. "Is Trump Trolling the White House Press Corps?" *New Yorker,* March 20. www.newyorker.com.

Markoe, Lauren. 2012. "Election 2012 Shows a Social Sea Change on Gay Marriage." *Huffington Post,* November 8. www.huffingtonpost.com.

Marshall, S. Alexandra, and M. Kathryn Allison. 2017. "Midwestern Misfits: Bullying Experienced by Perceived Sexual and Gender Minority Youth in the Midwestern United States." *Youth and Society,* 1–21. DOI: https://doi.org/10.1177/0044118X17697885.

Martin, Karin A., David J. Hutson, Emily Kazyak, and Kristin S. Scherrer. 2009. "Advice When Children Come Out: The Cultural 'Tool Kits' of Parents." *Journal of Family Issues* 31(7): 960–991.

Marx, Robert A., and Heather Hensman Kettrey. 2016. "Gay-Straight Alliances Are Associated with Lower Levels of School-Based Victimization of LGBTQ+ Youth: A Systematic Review and Meta-analysis." *Journal of Youth and Adolescence* 45: 1269–1282.

Mason-Schrock, Douglas 1996. "'Transsexuals' Narrative Construction of the True Self." *Social Psychology Quarterly* 59(3): 176–92.

McDermott, Elizabeth, Katrina Roen, and Jonathan Scourfield. 2008. "Avoiding Shame: Young LGBT People, Homophobia, and Self-Destructive Behaviors." *Culture, Health and Sexuality* 10(8): 815–829.

McDonald, Gary J. 1982. "Individual Differences in the Coming Out Process for Gay Men: Implications for Theoretical Models." *Journal of Homosexuality* 8(1): 47–59.

McIntosh, Mary. 1968. "The Homosexual Role." *Social Problems* 16(2): 182–192.

Meadow, Tey. 2011. "'Deep Down Where the Music Plays': How Parents Account for Childhood Gender Variance." *Sexualities* 14(6): 725–747.

———. 2018. *Trans Kids: Being Gendered in the Twenty-First Century*. Berkeley: University of California Press.

Mean Girls. 2004. Film, directed by Mark Waters, written by Tina Fey. Hollywood, CA: Paramount Pictures.

Meyer, Stephanie. 2005–2008. *Twilight* series. New York: Little, Brown.

Miceli, Melinda. 2005. *Standing Out, Standing Together: The Social and Political Impact of Gay-Straight Alliances*. New York: Routledge.

Mizoguchi, Akiko. 2010. "Theorizing Comics/Manga Genre as a Productive Forum: Yaoi and Beyond." In *Comics Worlds and the World of Comics: Towards Scholarship on a Global Scale*, edited by Jaqueline Berndt, 145–170. Kyoto: International Manga Research Center, Kyoto Seika University.

Moore, Mignon R. 2011. *Invisible Families: Gay Identities, Relationships, and Motherhood among Black Women*. Berkeley: University of California Press.

Muise, Amy. 2011. "Women's Sex Blogs: Challenging Dominant Discourses of Heterosexual Desire." *Feminism and Psychology* 21 (3): 411–419.

Muñoz, José Esteban. 2009. *Cruising Utopia: The Then and There of Queer Futurity*. New York: New York University Press.

Murdock, Tamera B., and Megan B. Bolch. 2005. "Risk and Protective Factors for Poor School Adjustment in Lesbian, Gay, and Bisexual (LGB) High School Youth: Variable and Person-Centered Analyses." *Psychology in the Schools* 42(2): 159–172.

Nagel, Joane. 2003. *Race, Ethnicity, and Sexuality: Intimate Intersections, Forbidden Frontiers*. New York: Oxford University Press.

Napier, Susan J. 2005. *Anime from "Akira" to "Howl's Moving Castle": Experiencing Contemporary Japanese Animation*. New York: Palgrave MacMillan.

Naples, Nancy. 2001. "A Member of the Funeral: An Introspective Ethnography." In *Queer Families, Queer Politics: Challenging Culture and the State*, edited by Mary Bernstein and Renate Reimann, 21–43. New York: Columbia University Press.

Neubeck, Kenneth J., and Noel A. Cazenave. 2001. *Welfare Racism: Playing the Race Card against America's Poor*. New York: Routledge.

Newman, Bernie Sue, and Peter Gerard Muzzonigro. 1993. "The Effects of Traditional Family Values on the Coming Out Process of Gay Male Adolescents." *Adolescence* 28(109): 213–226.

Nichols, James. 2013. "'Any Given Tuesday' Offers Stark Facts about Homeless LGBT Youth." *Huffington Post*, October 18. www.huffingtonpost.com.

North Carolina General Assembly. 2016. Second Extra Session, Session Law 2016-3, House Bill 2. Retrieved September 14, 2017. www.ncleg.net.

Ott, Miles Q., Heather L. Corliss, David Wypij, Margaret Rosario, and S. Bryn Austin. 2011. "Stability and Change in Self-Reported Sexual Orientation Identity in Young People: Application of Mobility Metrics." *Archives of Sexual Behavior* 40: 519–532.

Ouran High School Host Club. 2008. *Anime* series. English dub, DVD. Flower Mound, TX: Funimation Productions, 2012.

Overby, L. Marvin. 2014. "Etiology and Attitudes: Beliefs about the Origins of Homosexuality and Their Implications for Public Policy." *Journal of Homosexuality* 61(4): 568–587.

Padawer, Ruth. 2012. "What's So Bad about a Boy Who Wants to Wear a Dress?" *New York Times*, August 8. www.nytimes.com.

Parekh, Ranna. 2016. "What Is Gender Dysphoria?" February. American Psychiatric Association. www.psychiatry.org.

Parker-Pope, Tara. 2010. "Showing Gay Teenagers a Happy Future." *New York Times*, September 22. www.nytimes.com.

Pascoe, C. J. 2007. *Dude, You're a Fag: Masculinity and Sexuality in High School*. Berkeley: University of California Press.

———. 2011. "Resource and Risk: Youth Sexuality and New Media Use." *Sexual Research and Social Policy* 8: 5–17.

Penny, Laurie. 2017. "On the Milo Bus with the Lost Boys of America's New Right." *Pacific Standard*, February 21. https://psmag.com.

Peters, Jeremy W., Alexandra Alter, and Michael M. Grynbaum. 2017. "Milo Yiannopoulos's Pedophilia Comments Cost Him CPAC Role and Book Deal." *New York Times*, February 20. www.nytimes.com.

Peters, Jeremy W., Jo Becker, and Julie Hirschfeld Davis. 2017. "Trump Rescinds Rules on Bathrooms for Transgender Students." *New York Times*, February 22. www.nytimes.com.

Petrusich, Amanda. 2015. "Free to Be Miley." *Paper Magazine*, Summer. www.papermag.com.

Philadelphia. 1993. Film, directed by Jonathan Demme, written by Ron Nyswaner. Culver City, CA: TriStar Pictures.

Plummer, Kenneth. 1981. "Homosexual Categories: Some Research Problems in Labeling Perspective of Homosexuality." In *The Making of the Modern Homosexual*, edited by Kenneth Plummer, 53–75. London: Hutchinson.

Pollock, Lealah, and Stephen L. Eyre. 2012. "Growth into Manhood: Identity Development among Female-to-Male Transgender Youth." *Culture, Health and Sexuality* 14(2): 209–222.

Prensky, Marc. 2001. "Digital Natives, Digital Immigrants," pt. 1. *On the Horizon* 9(5): 1–6.

Preston, Julia, and John H. Cushman, Jr. 2012. "Obama to Permit Young Migrants to Remain in U.S." *New York Times*, June 15. www.nytimes.com.

Puar, Jasbir. 2005. "Queer Times, Queer Assemblages." *Social Text* 84–85(3–4): 121–139.

———. 2007. *Terrorist Assemblages: Homonationalism in Queer Times*. Durham, NC: Duke University Press.

Purcell, Kristen. 2013. "10 Things to Know about How Teens Use Technology." Pew Research Center, July 10. www.pewinternet.org.

Queer as Folk. 2000–2005. Television series. Burbank, CA: Warner Bros.

Ranma ½. 1989. *Anime* series. English dub. Vancouver, BC: Ocean Group.

Rich, Adrienne. 1980. "Compulsory Heterosexuality and Lesbian Existence." *Signs* 5(4): 631–660.

Rierson, Sandra. 2004. "Comstock Act (1873)." In *Major Acts of Congress*, edited by Brian K. Landsberg, 1: 166–169. New York: Macmillan Reference USA.

Risman, Barbara J. 1982. "The (Mis)Acquisition of Gender Identity among Transsexuals." *Qualitative Sociology* 5(4): 312–325.

Rivera, Syliva. 2002. "Queens in Exile, the Forgotten Ones." In *Gender Queer: Voices from beyond the Sexual Binary*, edited by Joan Nestle, Clare Howell, and Riki Wilchins, 67–85. Los Angeles: Alison Books.

Roberts, Andrea L., Margaret Rosario, Heather L. Corliss, Karestan C. Koenen, and S. Bryn Austin. 2012. "Elevated Risk of Posttraumatic Stress in Sexual Minority Youths: Mediation by Childhood Abuse and Gender Nonconformity." *American Journal of Public Health* 102(8): 1587–1593.

Roberts, Dorothy. 2002. *Shattered Bonds: The Color of Child Welfare*. New York: Civitas Books.

Rodríguez, Dylan. 2007. "The Political Logic of the Non-profit Industrial Complex." In *The Revolution Will Not Be Funded*, edited by INCITE! Women of Color Against Violence, 21–40. Cambridge, MA: South End Press.

Romijinders, Kim A., J. Michael Wilkerson, Rik Crutzen, Gerjo Kok, Jessica Bauldry, and Sylvia M. Lawler. 2017. "Strengthening Social Ties to Increase Confidence and Self-Esteem among Sexual and Gender Minority Youth." *Health Promotion Practice* 18(3): 341–347.

Roncero-Menendez, Sara. 2014. "Sailor Neptune and Uranus Come Out of the Fictional Closet." *Huffington Post*, May 21. www.huffingtonpost.com.

Rosario, Margaret, Eric W. Schrimshaw, Joyce Hunter, and Lisa Braun. 2006. "Sexual Identity Development among Lesbian, Gay, and Bisexual Youths: Consistency and Change over Time." *Journal of Sex Research* 43(1): 46–58.

Rosario, Margaret, Eric W. Schrimshaw, Joyce Hunter, Anna Levy-Warren. 2009. "The Coming Out Process of Young Lesbian and Bisexual Women: Are There Butch/ Femme Differences in Sexual Identity Development?" *Archives of Sexual Behavior* 38(1): 34–49.

Rowling, J. K. 1997–2007. *Harry Potter* series. New York: Scholastic.

Rubin, Gayle. 1984. "Thinking Sex: Notes for a Radical Theory of the Politics of Sexuality." In *Pleasure and Danger: Exploring Female Sexuality*, edited by Carol Vance, 3–44. Boston: Routledge & Kegan Paul.

RuPaul's Drag Race. 2009–present. Television show. Los Angeles: World of Wonder.

Russell, Stephen T., Thomas J. Clarke, and Justin Clary. 2009. "Are Teens 'Post-gay'? Contemporary Adolescents' Sexual Identity Labels." *Journal of Youth Adolescence* 38: 884–890.

Russo, Vito. 1981. *The Celluloid Closet*. New York: Quality Paperback Book Club.

Rust, Paula. 2003. "Bisexuality: The State of the Union." *Annual Review of Sex Research* 13: 180–240.

Saraswati, L Ayu. 2013. "Wikisexuality: Rethinking Sexuality in Cyberspace." *Sexualities* 16(5/6): 587–603.

Savage, Dan. 2015. "Not Gay Men Who Have Not Gay Sex with Other Not Gay Men." *Stranger*, July 27. www.thestranger.com.

Savin-Williams, Ritch C. 1998. "The Disclosure of Families of Same-Sex Attractions by Lesbian, Gay, and Bisexual Youths." *Journal of Research on Adolescence* 8(1): 49–68.

———. 2001. "Suicide Attempts among Sexual-Minority Youth: Population and Measurement Issues." *Journal of Consulting and Clinical Psychology* 69(6): 983–991.

———. 2005. *The New Gay Teenager*. Cambridge, MA: Harvard University Press.

———. 2011. "Identity Development among Sexual Minority Youth." In *Handbook of Identity Theory and Research*, 2 vols., edited by Seth J. Schwartz, Koen Luyckx, and Vivian L. Vignoles, 2:671–689. New York: Springer.

Savin-Williams, Ritch C., and Lisa M. Diamond. 2000. "Sexual Identity Trajectories among Sexual-Minority Youths: Gender Comparisons." *Archives of Sexual Behavior* 29(6): 607–627.

Savin-Williams, Ritch C., and Eric M. Dubé. 1998. "Parental Reactions to Their Child's Disclosure of a Gay/Lesbian Identity." *Family Relations* 47(1): 7–13.

Schilt, Kristen, and Laurel Westbrook. 2009. "Doing Gender, Doing Heteronormativity: 'Gender Normals,' Transgender People and the Social Maintenance of Heterosexuality." *Gender and Society* 23(4): 443–464.

———. 2015. "Bathroom Battlegrounds and Penis Panics." *Contexts* 14(3): 26–31.

Schwartz, John. 2012. *Oddly Normal: One Family's Struggle to Help Their Teenage Son Come to Terms with His Sexuality*. New York: Gotham Books.

Scodari, Christine, and Jenna L. Felder. 2000. "Creating a Pocket Universe: 'Shippers,' Fanfiction, and The X-Files Online." *Communication Studies* 51(Fall): 238–257.

Sean Saves the World. 2013–2014. Television show. New York: NBC Universal Television Distribution.

Sedgwick, Eve Kosofsky. 1991. "How to Bring Your Kids Up Gay." *Social Text* 29: 18–27.

Seidman, Steven. 1993. "Identity Politics in a 'Postmodern' Gay Culture: Some Historical and Conceptual Notes." In *Fear of a Queer Planet*, edited by Michael Warner, 105–142. Minneapolis: University of Minnesota Press.

———. 1994. *Beyond the Closet: The Transformation of Gay and Lesbian Life*. New York: Routledge.

Seidman, Steven, Chet Meeks, and Francie Traschen. 1999. "Beyond the Closet? The Changing Social Meaning of Homosexuality in the United States." *Sexualities* 2(1): 9–34.

Serano, Julia. 2007. *Whipping Girl: A Transsexual Woman on Sexism and the Scapegoating of Femininity.* Berkeley: Seal Press.

Shore, John. 2013. "Anti-gay Christianity Claims another Life." *Huffington Post,* July 17. www.huffingtonpost.com.

Shotwell, Alexis, and Trevor Sangrey. 2009. "Resisting Definition: Gendering through Interaction and Relational Selfhood." *Hypatia* 24(3): 56–76.

Silence of the Lambs. 1991. Film, directed by Jonathan Demme, written by Ted Tally. Los Angeles: Orion Pictures.

Six Feet Under. 2001–2005. Television series. Burbank, CA: Warner Bros.

Smith, Dorothy E. 1993. "The Standard North American Family: SNAF as an Ideological Code." *Journal of Family Issues* 14(1): 50–65.

Smith, Marshall. 2013. "Youth Viewing Sexually Explicit Material Online: Addressing the Elephant on the Screen." *Sexuality Research and Social Policy* 10(1): 62–75.

Soave, Robby. 2016. "Yes, Political Correctness Helped Elect Trump: What Skeptics Need to Know." *Reason Magazine,* December 19. http://reason.com.

Somogyi, Victoria. 2002. "Complexity of Desire: Janeway/Chakotay Fanfiction." *Journal of American and Comparative Cultures* 25(3–4): 399–405.

Southern Poverty Law Center. 2017. "Hate Groups Increase for Second Consecutive Year as Trump Electrifies Radical Right," February 15. www.splcenter.org.

Spade, Dean. 2011. *Normal Life: Administrative Violence, Critical Trans Politics, and the Limits of Law.* New York: South End Press.

SpongeBob SquarePants. 1999–present. Television show. Hollywood, CA: Paramount Television.

Stacey, Judith. 1993. "Good Riddance to 'The Family': A Response to David Popenoe." *Journal of Marriage and Family* 55(3): 545–547.

Stacey, Judith, and Timothy J. Biblarz. 2001. "(How) Does the Sexual Orientation of Parents Matter?" *American Sociological Review* 66(2): 159–183.

Star Trek. 1966–1969. Television series. Los Angeles: Desilu Productions; Hollywood, CA: Paramount Television.

Stein, Arlene. 1989. "Three Models of Sexuality: Drives, Identities and Practices." *Sociological Theory* 7(1): 1–13.

———. 2001. *The Stranger Next Door: The Story of a Small Community's Battle over Sex, Faith, and Civil Rights.* Boston: Beacon Press.

Stein, Edward. 1999. *The Mismeasure of Desire: The Science, Theory, and Ethics of Sexual Orientation.* Oxford: Oxford University Press.

———. 2012. "Commentary on the Treatment of Gender Variant and Gender Dysphoric Children and Adolescents: Common Themes and Ethnical Reflections." *Journal of Homosexuality* 59: 480–500.

Steinberg, Stephen. 2004. "The Melting Pot and the Color Line." In *Reinventing the Melting Pot: The New Immigrants and What It Means to Be American,* edited by Tamar Jacoby, 235–248. New York: Basic Books.

Stockton, Kathryn Bond. 2009. *The Queer Child, or Growing Sideways in the Twentieth Century.* Durham, NC: Duke University Press.

Stoler, Ann Laura. 1995. *Race and the Education of Desire: Foucault's History of Sexuality and the Colonial Order of Things.* Durham, NC: Duke University Press.

Stone, Sandy. 1991. "The Empire Strikes Back: A Posttranssexual Manifesto." In *Bodyguards: The Cultural Politics of Gender Ambiguity,* edited by Julia Epstein and Kristina Straub, 280–304. New York: Routledge.

Striepe, Meg I., and Deborah L. Tolman. 2003. "Mom, Dad, I'm Straight: The Coming Out of Gender Ideologies in Adolescent Sexual-Identity Development." *Journal of Clinical Child and Adolescent Psychology* 32(4): 523–530.

Stryker, Susan. 2006. "(De)Subjugated Knowledges: An Introduction to Transgender Studies." In *The Transgender Studies Reader,* edited by Susan Stryker and Stephen Whittle, 1–17. New York: Routledge.

———. 2007. "Transgender Feminism: Queering the Woman Question." In *Third Wave Feminism,* edited by Stacy Gillis, Gillian Howie, and Rebecca Mumford, 59–70. New York: Palgrave MacMillan.

———. 2008. *Transgender History.* Berkeley, CA: Seal Press.

Stryker, Susan, and Paisley Currah. 2014. "Introduction." *TSQ: Transgender Studies Quarterly* 1(1–2): 1–18.

Supernatural. 2005–present. Television show. Burbank, CA: Warner Bros.

Teen Wolf. 2011–present. Television show. New York: Viacom Media Networks.

Thorn, Matt. 2004. "Girls and Women Getting Out of Hand: The Pleasure and Politics of Japan's Amateur Comics Community." In *Fanning the Flames: Fans and Consumer Culture in Contemporary Japan,* edited by William W. Kelley, 169–187. Albany, NY: SUNY Press.

Tolman, Deborah L., and Sara I. McClelland. 2009. "Normative Sexuality Development in Adolescence: A Decade in Review, 2000–2009." *Journal of Research on Adolescence* 21(1): 242–255.

Travers, Ann. 2018. *The Trans Generation: How Trans Kids (and Their Parents) Are Creating a Gender Revolution.* New York: New York University Press.

Troiden, Richard R. 1979. "Becoming Homosexual: A Model of Gay Identity Acquisition." *Psychiatry* 42: 362–373.

———. 1989. "The Formation of Homosexual Identities." *Journal of Homosexuality* 17(1/2): 43–73.

U.S. Department of Health and Human Services. 2009. Code of Federal Regulations, Title 45, Public Welfare, Department of Health and Human Services, Part 46, Protection of Human Subjects. Washington, DC: U.S. Department of Health and Human Services. Revised January 15, 2009. www.hhs.gov.

U.S. Department of Justice. 2016. "Justice Department Files Complaint against the State of North Carolina to Stop Discrimination against Transgender Individuals." Washington, DC: U.S. Department of Justice, Office of Public Affairs, May 9. www.justice.gov.

Usher, Raven, ed. 2006. *North American Lexicon of Transgender Terms.* San Francisco: GLB Publishers.

Vance, Carol. 1989. "Social Construction Theory: Problems in the History of Sexuality."
In *Homosexuality, Which Homosexuality?* edited by A. van Kooten Nierkerk and T.
van Der Meer, 13–34. Amsterdam: An Dekker.

Valentine, David. 2004. "The Categories Themselves." *GLQ: A Journal of Lesbian and
Gay Studies* 10(2): 215–220.

———. 2007. *Imagining Transgender: An Ethnography of a Category.* Durham, NC:
Duke University Press.

van Anders, Sari M. 2013. "Beyond Masculinity: Testosterone, Gender/Sex, and Human
Social Behavior in a Comparative Context." *Frontiers in Neuroendocrinology* 34(3):
198–210.

———. 2015. "Beyond Sexual Orientation: Integrating Gender/Sex and Diverse Sexualities via Sexual Configurations Theory." *Archives of Sexual Behavior* 44: 1177–1213.

Van Leeuwen, James M., Susan Boyle, Stacy Salomonsen-Sautel, D. Nico Baker, J. T.
Garcia, Allison Hoffman, and Christian J. Hopfer. 2005. "Lesbian, Gay, and Bisexual
Homeless Youth: An Eight-City Public Health Perspective." *Child Welfare* 8(2):
151–170.

Vidal-Ortiz, Salvador. 2002. "Queering Sexuality and Doing Gender: Transgender
Men's Identification with Gender and Sexuality." *Sexualities* 6: 181–233.

———. 2008. "Teaching and Learning Guide for: Transgender and Transsexual Studies:
Sociology's Influence and Future Steps." *Sociology Compass* 2(2): 799–807.

Voisin, Dexter R., Jason D. P. Bird, Cheng-Shi Shiu, and Cathy Krieger. 2013. "'It's
Crazy Being a Black, Gay Youth.' Getting Information about HIV Prevention: A
Pilot Study." *Journal of Adolescence* 36(1): 111–119.

Wade, Lisa. 2013. "The New Science of Sex Difference." *Sociology Compass* 7(4):
274–293.

Waidzunas, Tom. 2012. "Young, Gay, and Suicidal: Dynamic Nominalism and the Process of Defining a Social Problem with Statistics." *Science, Technology, and Human
Values* 37(2): 199–225.

———. 2015. *The Straight Line: How the Fringe Science of Ex-gay Therapy Reoriented
Sexuality.* Minneapolis: University of Minnesota Press.

Walls, N. Eugene, Sarah B. Kane, and Hope Wisneski. 2010. "Gay-Straight Alliances and School Experiences of Sexual Minority Youth." *Youth and Society* 41(3):
307–332.

Walls, N. Eugene, Julie Laser, Sarah J. Nickels, and Hope Wisneski. 2010. "Correlates of
Cutting Behavior among Sexual Minority Youths and Young Adults." *Social Work
Research* 34(4): 213–226.

Walsh, Bill. 2015. "The *Post* Drops the 'Mike'—and the Hyphen in 'E-mail.'" *Washington
Post*, December 4. www.washingtonpost.com.

Warner, Michael, ed. 1993. *Fear of a Queer Planet: Queer Politics and Social Theory.*
Minneapolis: University of Minnesota Press.

———. 2000. *The Trouble with Normal: Sex, Politics, and the Ethics of Queer Life.* Boston, MA: Harvard University Press.

Ward, Jane. 2008. *Respectably Queer: Diversity Culture in LGBT Activist Organizations.* Nashville, TN: Vanderbilt University Press.

———. 2015. *Not Gay: Sex between Straight White Men.* New York: New York University Press.

Weber, Mathias, Oliver Quiring, and Gregor Daschmann. 2012. "Peers, Parents and Pornography: Exploring Adolescents' Exposure to Sexually Explicit Material and Its Developmental Correlates." *Sexuality and Culture* 16(4): 408–427.

Weeks, Jeffrey. 1985. *Sexuality and Its Discontents: Meanings, Myths, and Modern Sexualities.* London: Routledge & Kegan Paul.

Welker, James. 2006. "Beautiful, Borrowed, and Bent: 'Boys' Love' as Girls' Love in *Shôjo Manga.*" *Signs: Journal of Women in Culture and Society* 31(3): 841–870.

Weinberg, Thomas S. 1978. "On 'Doing' and 'Being' Gay: Sexual Behavior and Homosexual Male Self-Identity." *Journal of Homosexuality* 4(2): 143–156.

Weinrich, James D. 1997. "Strange Bedfellows: Homosexuality, Gay Liberation, and the Internet." *Journal of Sex Education and Therapy* 22 (1): 58–66.

West, Candace, and Don H. Zimmerman. 1987. "Doing Gender." *Gender and Society* 1(2): 125–151.

———. 2009. "Accounting for Doing Gender." *Gender and Society* 23(1): 112–122.

Westbrook, Laurel, and Kristen Schilt. 2013. "Doing Gender, Determining Gender: Transgender People, Gender Panics, and the Maintenance of the Sex/Gender/Sexuality System." *Gender and Society* 28(1): 32–57.

Weston, Kath. 1991. *Families We Choose: Lesbians, Gays, Kinship.* New York: Columbia University Press.

Whisman, Vera. 1996. *Queer by Choice: Lesbians, Gay Men, and the Politics of Identity.* New York: Routledge.

Whittier, Nancy. 1994. "Reviewed Work(s): Children of Horizons: How Gay and Lesbian Teens Are Leading a New Way Out of the Closet. By Gilbert Herdt and Andrew Boxer." *Contemporary Sociology* 23(2): 289–290.

Will & Grace. 1998–2006. Television show. New York: NBC Studios.

Williams, Cristan. 2014. "Transgender." *TSQ: Transgender Studies Quarterly* 1(1–2): 232–234.

Wright, Eric R., and Brea L. Perry. 2006. "Sexual Identity Distress, Social Support, and the Health of Gay, Lesbian, and Bisexual Youth." *Journal of Homosexuality* 51(1): 81–110.

INDEX

ability/disability: identity formation and, 5–6, 25, 44, 56; marginalization and, 144; queerness and, 58
abstinence-only policies, 41, 160n9
abuse, in families, 120–21
acceptance, 40, 132, 137
activism. *See* civil rights movements; LGBTQ rights movement; social justice movements
adolescent sexuality, fluidity of, 23–24. *See also* fluidity; sexual identity formation
adults, 16–17, 38–39, 96. *See also* LGBTQ resource centers; parents
Against Me! (rock band), 72
Ahmed, Sara, 5–6, 46–47, 147; *Queer Phenomenology*, 68, 159n3
alternative family forms. *See* families: nontraditional
alternative media, 25–26; representations of queerness in, 91–92, 96. *See also* mainstream media; queer media
Altman, Dennis, 160n12
alt-right movement, 42–44
ambiguity, 143, 152. *See also* gender ambiguity
ambivalence, 23–24, 80–81
American Couples (Blumstein and Schwartz), 170n22
American Psychological Association, 76
androgyny, 59, 73, 81, 88
anime (Japanese animation), 5, 26, 96, 104–8; erotic, 108–14
Anime clubs, 108
Asian population, 32

at-risk narrative. *See* risk

Baldwin, Tammy, 40
"bathroom bills," 41–42, 87, 146
Battle, Juan, 120
BDSM (bondage, discipline, and sadomasochism), 58
becoming, process of. *See* identity formation
behavior. *See* sexual behavior
Bennett, Michael, 120
Beyond the Closet (Seidman), 163n8
Biblarz, Timothy J., 131
bigotry, 41, 149. *See also* homophobia
binary categories, 139–40; conflation of sexuality and gender, 71–72, 81, 128; gender, 11–12, 25, 27, 46, 69–73, 76, 88–89, 121; sexuality, 25, 27, 64–66, 139; transbinary, 166n26
bioessentialism. *See* essentialism
biracial youth, 62, 84, 107, 109. *See also* multiracial youth
The Bird Cage (film), 102
birth certificates, 87–88, 166n28, 169n8
bisexual, use of term, 22
bisexual parents, 118
bisexual youth, 15, 48, 51–52, 54–55, 59, 62, 83–84, 94–95, 107, 125, 130, 150
Black, Rebecca, 110
Black family, 120, 168n5
Black LGBTQ people, 120, 168n9
Black Lives Matter movement, 27, 148, 151. *See also* social justice movements
Black population, 32

ABOUT THE AUTHOR

Mary Robertson is Assistant Professor of Sociology at California State University San Marcos.